T0266743

EDITOR'S LETTER

Joining Ukraine's battle for freedom

We need to support the new dissidents fighting Putin's war of fear and propaganda, writes **JEMIMAH STEINFELD**

RUSSIA'S INVASION OF Ukraine at the end of February pitted a pluralistic society with liberal values and a straight-talking leader against a country synonymous with autocracy that has a "strongman" at the helm. People started talking about a New Cold War – not just because it involved Russia again but because it centred on values and ideals. Ukraine became a symbol of freedom, Russia one of illiberalism.

That said Vladimir Putin's war has been far from cold and ultimately historical comparisons come with limitations. Understanding the new terms, documenting the unfolding abuses to free expression and supporting those being attacked is paramount.

This is the focus of our summer edition. In our special report, people across the spectrum talk about the corrosive effect of the war on their own freedoms. Viktória Serdült, a journalist in Hungary, writes about how Europe's most right-wing leader, Prime Minister Viktor Orbán, used fears of being embroiled in the war to secure a resounding electoral victory. Hanna Komar, an activist from Belarus, tells how she is desperately trying to

challenge her parents on the lies they see on their TV. These lies could lead young men and women to enlist in the war and must be called out.

We give space to Ukrainian writers and artists, with a moving essay from Andrey Kurkov on how today, as in the past, Russia is trying to erase Ukraine's culture, and a discussion with the poet Lyuba Yakimchuk on children in Donbas being fed an alternative history.

Of course, when it comes to censorship Russia remains ground zero. The passage of the "fake news" law straight after the invasion showed that. And so we have several articles from those brave enough to make a stand. We publish the court statement from student journalist Alla Gutnikova, one of the Doxa Four sentenced to two years' "correctional labour" in April, alongside an interview with her. Ilya Matveev, a Russian academic, writes about the incredibly difficult environment in his St Petersburg classroom, which eventually led him to flee.

You'll also find the powerful words of murdered Russian journalist Anna Politkovskaya, reporting from Chechnya in 1999. Her warnings and experience of early Putin warfare

resonate more today than ever and deserve a bigger audience.

We are aware of the sensitivities of publishing Russian and Ukrainian writers next to each other (and have invited two writers from opposite camps to debate the very thorny issue of the cultural boycott of Russian artists). But, to quote Polish poet Adam Mickiewicz in his poem To My Russian Friends: "As for those of you who are complicit, it is not you that I want to destroy, but your shackles."

We are also aware that while Europe witnesses its first major war since the 1990s, attacks on freedoms continue elsewhere – only somewhat less reported. Please read the harrowing testimony of Uyghur "re-education" camp survivor Gulbahar Haitiwaji, and an interview with the writer Eduardo Halfon, who doesn't mince his words on the horrendous rights situation in Guatemala. Halfon describes the country's history as one of "silence", something which is being repeated today. As always, it remains our duty to fill that silence. ✖

Jemimah Steinfeld is Index editor

51(02):1/1|DOI:10.1177/03064220221110703

Art is eternal

About our cover illustration

Irina Potapenko is from Odessa. She says, "For many years I have been illustrating books for children and adults and painting watercolours. When the war started, I began to paint it too as I wanted to tell people all over the world about it. Bombs and rockets destroy our cities, forcing me and my husband to hide in the basement with our pets. Painting helps me maintain mental strength. With this illustration, I wanted to show that cities get ruined but art is eternal."

CONTENTS

The Index

51(02):4/12|DOI:10.1177/03064220221110705

A round-up of events in the world of free expression from Index's unparalleled network of writers and activists

Edited by
MARK FRARY

PICTURED: A Palestinian artist paints a mural in honour of slain Al Jazeera journalist Shireen Abu Akleh in Gaza City on 12 May 2022, the day after she was killed. Abu Akleh was shot while covering an Israeli raid in the occupied West Bank town of Jenin. The journalist was known for her balanced coverage of the Israeli-Palestinian conflict. As yet no one has been held officially accountable. A Palestinian investigation concluded she was intentionally shot by an Israeli soldier, but Israel's defence minister called the report "a blatant lie".

CREDIT: Majdi Fathi/NurPhoto/Getty

The Index

ELECTION WATCH

GUILHERME OSINSKI looks at what is happening at the poll booths of the world

1. Philippines

9 MAY

In May, the Philippines elected a dictator's son to run the country. The new president is Ferdinand "Bongbong" Marcos Jr, whose father was the notorious Ferdinand Marcos, a dictator who ruled over the country between 1965 and 1986.

In his speech after his electoral victory, Marcos Jr said "judge me not by my ancestors, but by my actions", perhaps an attempt to distance himself from his father's legacy. However, during his campaign he used the slogan "together we shall rise again", hinting at a return to former greatness that many understood as a reference to his father. On his first official day as president, he only invited three reporters, from SMNI, NET25 and GMA News, to a press conference. SMNI and NET25's owners openly supported Marcos Jr's campaign.

He leads with vice-president Sara Duterte, daughter of former President Rodrigo Duterte, who was the leader from 2016 through to 2022. Under his leadership, human rights and media freedom severely deteriorated.

2. Angola

24 AUGUST

Tensions are building in Angola as the general election scheduled for August approaches. João Lourenço, the current president, is seeking re-election as head of the People's Movement for the Liberation of Angola, a party that has run the country since 1975.

Lourenço is expected to be challenged by the National Union for the Total Independence of Angola (Unita), who joined forces with other opposition parties to create the Patriotic Front, with Adalberto Costa Júnior chosen as their candidate.

Angola has been facing an economic crisis due to its dependence on oil exports and an increase in prices. To make things worse, there are concerns about the election's transparency - Lourenço has proposed a bill to centralise the counting of votes, which is usually done by each county and province.

There have also been crackdowns on peaceful protesters. In April, 22 people were arrested in Luanda for taking to the streets to call for free elections.

3. Kenya

9 AUGUST

As Kenya once again prepares to go to the polls, there are fears it could be similar to the 2017 elections, which were marred by intense ethnic violence. With incumbent President Uhuru Kenyatta not eligible to run for a third term, the contest is likely to be between William Ruto from the United Democratic Alliance party and Kenyatta's vice president, and Raila Odinga, from the Orange Democratic Movement.

In 2017, Odinga lost to Kenyatta but claimed polling results were manipulated and that the electoral system had been hacked and was rife with fraud. As soon as word spread that Kenyatta was re-elected, violence and protests scaled up. There were numerous human rights violations, with some people killed.

Kenyatta and Ruto have also had a bitter fall-out and are no longer presenting a common face as they did when they were first elected. At the beginning of May, Ruto accused Kenyatta of not convening a cabinet meeting for two years.

The Kenyan people don't really trust the country's electoral management body, the Independent Electoral and Boundaries Commission, who were blamed for the post-election violence that took over in 2017. ✖

THE LATEST FROM OUR CAMPAIGNS

INDEX ON CENSORSHIP works on a number of active campaigns around the world. Find out more at indexoncensorship.org

Online Safety Bill will "significantly curtail freedom of expression"

The proposed Online Safety Bill has simple, laudable aims – to make the online sphere safer. But despite almost seven years of debate, thousands of hours of parliamentary scrutiny, analysis from civil society, business and the media, there is still significant uncertainty about how the bill will work in practice.

To fill this gap and help explain what the bill will mean in practice, the Legal to Say, Legal to Type campaign, which includes Index, has instructed media law expert Gavin Millar QC of Matrix Chambers to produce the first analysis of the implications of the Online Safety Bill on UK citizens' freedom of speech.

The QC's opinion explains and analyses the broad implications of the government's new online safety regime against current freedom of expression laws and found that the bill will significantly curtail freedom of expression in a way that has profound consequences for the British media and journalism, courts and the UK's digital economy. The bill gives the Secretary of State overseeing the legislation unprecedented powers to curtail freedom of expression with limited parliamentary scrutiny.
Read the QC's report at
tinyurl.com/Index512OSB

Attacks on journalists covering protests increase

Physical attacks on journalists have increased dramatically over the past year, according to the latest annual report from the Council of Europe (CoE) Platform on media freedom in Europe.

The platform, of which Index on Censorship is a partner, reports on serious threats to the safety of journalists and media freedom in Europe in order to reinforce the CoE's response to the threats and member states' accountability.

The new report, Defending Press Freedom in Times of Tension and Conflict, reveals that the number of cases involving the safety and physical integrity of journalists has jumped by 51% year-on-year, with 82 cases reported to the platform.

Many of the attacks on journalists have taken place during public protests.

"Violence against journalists during street protests is fed by a wave of media bashing and an avalanche of hate speech on social networks – very often prompted by political figures – which directly target journalists, questioning their independence and legitimacy and therefore making them more vulnerable to physical aggression," the report says.

Overall, the number of alerts in all categories published by the CoE platform has sky-rocketed to 280 in 2021, up from around 200 in 2020 and more than double the level reported in 2016. Of the 280 alerts, 110 related to the harassment and intimidation of journalists.
Read more on the report at **tinyurl.com/Index512COE** ✖

Ink spot

Cartoonists **GÀBOR PÀPAI** from Hungary and **VLADIMIR KAZANEVSKY** from Ukraine have won the 2022 Kofi Annan Courage in Cartooning Award

PATRICK CHAPPATTE, PRESIDENT of the Freedom Cartoonists Foundation, said at the May award ceremony in Geneva: "We are particularly proud to present them with the Kofi Annan Courage in Cartooning Award in the presence of prominent journalists and co-laureates of the Nobel Peace Prize, Maria Ressa and Dmity Muratov: they all share a strong sense of justice and a will to resist. Cartoonists do it through their art and take huge risks in showing the emperor is naked and in depicting the full brutality of autocrats."

Pàpai works for the only remaining opposition newspaper in Hungary Népszava, which has been the subject of attacks and legal proceedings by the authorities.

Pàpai continues to critically observe and draw all political actors in Hungary and beyond.

This cartoon shows his take on the evolution of man.

The Index

PEOPLE WATCH

GUILHERME OSINSKI highlights the stories of human rights defenders under attack

Jasã Jenull

SLOVENIA

Jasã Jenull is a theatre director and activist from Slovenia who got into hot water after engaging in peaceful protests in the country against outgoing Prime Minister Janez Janša and his government. Jenull has denied being behind the protests but faces the possibility of paying thousands in legal costs.

According to Amnesty International, these arbitrary actions seek to intimidate and constrain other demonstrators, as well as silencing and putting a financial strain on people fighting for human rights.

Oleg Orlov

RUSSIA

On 6 March 2022, Oleg Orlov, member of the Council of the Human Rights Center Memorial, was arrested after attending a peaceful protest against the war in Ukraine. He was charged with "violating the established procedure" for a demonstration. Following a 10 hour detention, he was released but was fined.

A month later, Orlov was arrested again due to another anti-war demonstration. Even though he was set free on the same day, he could be sentenced to five years in jail.

Olena Shevchenko

UKRAINE

Olena Shevchenko, an important LGBTQI and women's rights voice in Ukraine, was forced to leave Kyiv for Lviv when Russia invaded.

On 14 April 2022, Shevchenko was assaulted by two unidentified individuals who threw tear gas on her face, burning her face, eyes and hands. She later reported it to the police.

Harassing LGBTQI people is not something new in Ukraine. Shevchenko herself has already been a victim, when two men beat her in Kyiv in 2019 while yelling homophobic words.

Irina Danilovich

CRIMEA

On 29 April 2022, human rights defender Irina Danilovich was abducted in Koktebel, Crimea as she returned home from work. Police told her father that she had "transferred unclassified information to a foreign state".

Danilovich has spoken out about the response of the healthcare system during Covid and been labelled a foreign agent. At the time of going to press, she was being held in a detention centre in Crimea's capital, Simferopol where she faces up to eight years in prison.

'We feel responsible for the future of Russophone culture'

Russian art historian DENIS STOLYAROV is assistant curator at Pushkin House, an independent cultural centre in London

During a historical catastrophe a cultural institution has to reinvent itself. After Russia invaded Ukraine, Pushkin House handed over its social media accounts to artists from Ukraine for them to share their experiences of the war. Several artists took up this opportunity, including Olia Fedorova, Anton Karyuk, Mykyta Lyskov and Kateryna Lysovenko.

As an independent cultural organisation, we feel responsible for the future of Russophone culture and it is our duty to create opportunities for people in the UK to express solidarity with Ukraine. We have platformed those voices that speak out effectively against the war. One of the most impressive oppositional forces that has appeared recently in

Russia is the Feminist Anti-War Resistance. Pushkin House has organised a panel discussion with one of its coordinators, Ella Rossman. A new political movement is being shaped that amasses tens of thousands of participants. Pushkin House has also organised several successful fundraising events, including an art sale at the end of March. It contributed towards the

financial security of Yellow Fields Blue Skies, a grassroot initiative that provides psychological support to women and children displaced in Ukraine.

Given the Russian state's crackdown on independent thinking inside the country, it is crucial for us in London to use our free voice as an institution and promote this important collective anti-war message.

BANNED BOOKS WATCH

Assistant editor **KATIE DANCEY-DOWNS** looks at the three most challenged books in the USA as identified by the American Library Association

Gender Queer: A Memoir

BY MAIA KOBABE

In this graphic novel, Kobabe, who uses e/em/eir pronouns, takes us on a visual journey through eir own journey of gender identity. E explores topics like first kisses, the importance of names, and who's allowed to remove their shirt at the beach. Kobabe wrote the book not only for teens, but for eir own family, who struggled to get to grips with what it means to be non-binary.

This autobiography faced such strong opposition that it landed the spot of most banned book in the USA last year, being removed from specific libraries and classrooms across multiple states.

Like many others in the top 10, the censor's pen was wielded due to LGBT content. South Carolina Governor Henry McMaster wrote a letter to the department of education saying the book contained "sexually explicit and pornographic depictions, which easily meet or exceed the statutory definition of obscenity".

All Boys Aren't Blue

BY GEORGE M JOHNSON

Journalist and activist George M Johnson, who uses they/them pronouns, recounts their experiences of race and sexuality in this memoir. They lay out memories and explore their identity through a collection of essays, showing what it's like growing up in New Jersey as a Black, queer person. The book deals with bullying, consent, and in one scene, Johnson recounts an experience of sexual assault that they experienced as a child.

Libraries and classrooms in a number of states removed the book from their shelves, following complaints that it contained sexually explicit material.

Moms for Liberty, one of the groups spearheading the campaign for the book to be banned nationwide, tweeted: "They [school board members] want to rob children of their innocence." Multiple reviews on Amazon condemn the book with one word: "Porn!"

Lawn Boy

BY JONATHAN EVISON

This American Dream story follows Mike Munoz, a young gay man who is on a journey of discovery, trying desperately to get ahead in the world.

Like the other books in the most-banned line up, this semi-autobiographical novel was taken off shelves for its LGBT content and sexually explicit material. One of the offending passages describes a sexual encounter between two primary school aged boys. In Leander, Texas, police are even investigating the book being in school libraries.

On Instagram, Evison wrote: "I have received a number of threats to my health this week, because a lady in Texas is on a crusade to get Lawn Boy banned, because it features a gay protagonist who has had gay life experiences."

Florida Governor Ron DeSantis has since signed a bill that allows parents to search lists of books available in schools, and to object. He specifically referenced Lawn Boy as containing passages of "paedophilia". ✖

  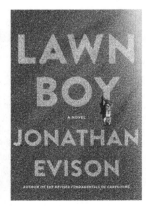

The Index

World In Focus: Ethiopia

War erupted in the northern Ethiopian region of Tigray in November 2020 after clashes between troops loyal to Prime Minister Abiy Ahmed and local leaders who fear Ahmed wants to recentralise power

1 Addis Ababa
CAPITAL CITY

On 1 May 2022, eight armed men raided the residence of editor and founder of the privately-owned YouTube-based broadcaster Voice of Amhara, Gobeze Sisay, abducting him, and holding and questioning him for eight days.

During his detention, Sisay was repeatedly questioned about his critical reporting and affiliations with opposition political groups and was warned to stop such reporting or they would detain him again.

Sisay told the Committee to Protect Journalists on his release that he believed some of the men were members of the Ethiopian National Defense Force.

Angela Quintal, CPJ's Africa programme coordinator, said:

"Instead of arresting reporters, the government must act swiftly to expose those within its ranks who seek to silence and harass the press, and should publicly commit to ensuring that all journalists can work safely without fear of arrest or prosecution."

2 Oromia
REGIONAL STATE

On 6 April 2022 Tamerat Negera Feyisa, co-founder and editor of the Terara Network online news outlet, was released on bail

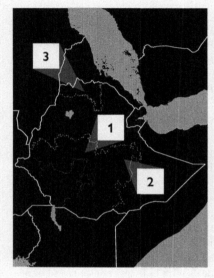

but only after spending four months in a detention facility in Oromia regional state.

Tamerat was arrested on 10 December 2021 as part of a nationwide state of emergency declared a month earlier, which had seen 14 journalists detained, according to the CPJ.

It is believed he was detained for alleged dissemination of disinformation, smearing the name of Oromia regional state, and defaming senior Ethiopian government officials including Prime Minister Abiy Ahmed Ali.

However, the journalist was not charged with any crime during those four months.

3 Tigray
NATIONAL REGIONAL STATE

The Ethiopian Human Rights Commission said it is investigating a video which has been circulating on social media, showing fighters in the Ethiopian army uniform abusing and shooting a young boy from Tigray. The soldiers taunted, kicked and stoned the boy before shooting him in the stomach.

Reuters reported that one solider said, "Don't kill him, let him suffer," while another said: "He can't talk now, we were first supposed to get information from him."

The soldiers then force banknotes into the boy's mouth and threaten to bury him alive.

In April, Amnesty International and Human Rights Watch released a report stating that administrators in the Western Tigray zone, as well as regional officials and security forces from Ethiopia's Amhara region, are responsible for a campaign of ethnic cleansing, carried out through crimes against humanity and war crimes, targeting Tigrayan civilians in Western Tigray.

Our first and founding editor writes...

Dear Editor,

Congratulations on producing such a compendious edition of Index to celebrate the magazine's 50th anniversary. Its articles shine a bright light on the practice of censorship over the past half-century. I was surprised however to see you have set your new account of Index's history, Dissidents, Spies, and the Lies that Came in from the Cold, for which I was interviewed, in the context of the Cold War. We were not fighting the Cold War in the period you mention, nor did we have any truck with outfits such as the CIA, which was the business of statesmen and politicians, not crusaders for human rights. What Index fought was censorship (as the author, Martin Bright, correctly notes) all over the world, and in the name of freedom of expression, a human right that transcended wars and was violated on all sides. It may sound like a small distinction, but is an important one, and explains, among other things, why Index is still here.

Michael Scammell, *Founding editor of Index on Censorship*

TECH WATCH: ELON MUSK'S ON-OFF TWITTER DEAL

MARK FRARY on the free speech future of a Musk Twitter

ON 25 APRIL, Twitter announced that it had entered into a definitive agreement to be acquired by an entity wholly owned by the world's richest man, tech entrepreneur Elon Musk, in a transaction valued at approximately $44 billion.

Musk has hinted for several years that he might be interested in buying the platform. In the announcement, Musk was quick to outline his plans for the platform, making freedom of expression activists nervous. He said: "Free speech is the bedrock of a functioning democracy, and Twitter is the digital town square where matters vital to the future of humanity are debated. I also want to make Twitter better than ever by enhancing the product with new features, making the algorithms open source to increase trust, defeating the spam bots, and authenticating all humans."

Musk describes himself as a "free speech absolutist", posting that he would not remove access to Russian news sources through his satellite internet company Starlink, "except at gunpoint". He later clarified his position on free speech, saying: "By "free speech", I simply mean that which matches the law. I am against censorship that goes far beyond the law. If people want less free speech, they will ask government to pass laws to that effect. Therefore, going beyond the law is contrary to the will of the people."

There was speculation that Musk's acquisition would see him reinstate Donald Trump to the platform. The former president was permanently banned from Twitter on 8 January 2021 "due to the risk of further incitement of violence" following the storming of the US Capitol by his supporters. Trump himself says he won't rejoin, even though his own platform is struggling.

The commitment of Twitter's other investors to free speech is also worth considering. Saudi Arabia's Prince Alwaleed bin Talal Al Saud owns 5.2% of Twitter through personal holdings and through Kingdom Holding. He initially rejected Musk's offer, saying it undervalued the company.

Digital civil rights organisation Access Now wrote an open letter to Twitter shareholders and financial institutions looking to back the deal calling for it to be examined in more detail. The signatories said, "Twitter's content moderation policies, which have been put in place to ensure user protection, are at risk under Elon Musk's leadership. In fact, Musk appears to view these policies as a form of censorship and is reportedly considering measures to weaken these protections."

In early June, Musk's lawyers wrote to Twitter accusing it of not providing sufficient detail on its false users and threatening to terminate the deal. ✖

Free speech in numbers

18

Length of sentence in years to be served by seven Gezi Park protesters in Turkey. Human rights activist Osman Kavala faces life imprisonment

6

Official number of reported deaths from Covid-19 in North Korea, far below what health experts believe

40

The number of journalists killed carrying out their jobs in 2022, according to the CPJ

264.4

The estimated wealth in billions of US dollars of Twitter suitor Elon Musk

49

The number of years since the US Supreme Court decided that the Constitution of the United States protects a pregnant woman's freedom to choose to have an abortion without excessive government restriction, a decision it is now expected to overturn

The Index

TO THINK, TO EXPRESS, TO BE

MY INSPIRATION

BBC presenter **SANA SAFI** pays tribute to her fellow Afghan journalists, who continue to
report the news despite ongoing human-rights violations by the Taliban

THE FIRST THING I do when I wake up every day is check the growing WhatsApp, Signal and Telegram groups on my phone. I see picture after picture of beaten and bruised men, women in distress and, sometimes, dead bodies.

Then I open Twitter to see what Afghans have shared on groups there. Again, I'm flooded with pictures and videos of men, women and children running after a loaf of bread, men being tied to a pole or held by four others while being tortured or women protesting yet another violation of their rights.

Then I open my Apple News app and click on the word "Afghanistan" – which I've followed as a topic – just to see if any of the user-generated content has been verified by any mainstream media or what stories have been written from or about the country. About 95% of what I read on the app is written by non-Afghan journalists or Afghans who now live in exile. This is because, since the Taliban regained power in August 2021, many journalists have left Afghanistan or are no longer in the profession.

According to a report by the International Federation of Journalists published in February 2022, only 305 out of 623 media outlets remain active in Afghanistan following the Taliban takeover. There were up to 6,000 journalists before August 2021; that figure is now 2,334. Female journalists are most affected – only 243 of the 979 women are still in their jobs.

On top of that, the Taliban

ABOVE: Prince Charles talks with Sana Safi BBC Afghan senior presenter while visiting the TV studio at BBC Broadcasting House in London, April 2022

authorities have introduced several measures which Afghan journalists say increasingly restrict their ability to do their jobs. New guidelines from the Vice and Virtue Ministry ordered female TV presenters and other women on screen to cover their faces while on air. Previous decrees issued by the same ministry prohibited soap operas and entertainment programmes featuring female actors.

Friends, colleagues and ordinary Afghans I talk to about what's happening – especially regarding the media – are worried. They are worried about not being able to access free and impartial news, anxious about being cut off from the rest of the world, and concerned about what this means for their rights to think, to express and even to be.

What gives me hope and inspires me every day are the men and women in Afghanistan who, despite all the difficulties and increasing restrictions from the de-facto authorities, remain committed to delivering the sort of free and fair news that Afghans so desperately need. ✖

Sana Safi is a senior presenter of BBC Pashto's TV news programme BBC Naray Da Wakht (BBC World Right Now)

FEATURES

"Today a Muslim feels insecure when he runs a dhaba
(a small eatery); a Muslim feels insecure ferrying
cattle; a Muslim feels insecure offering prayers"

AISHWARYA JAGANI SPEAKS TO INDIAN MUSLIMS ABOUT HOW AN ESCALATION IN
PERSECUTION HAS REACHED THE DINNER TABLE | INDIA'S MEATY ISSUE, P.17

Fifty years of Pride and prejudice

Pride started as a way to give voice to the silenced, but it lost its way. Ahead of its 50th anniversary, a new protest movement has emerged, writes **PETER TATCHELL**

BRITAIN'S FIRST LGBT+ Pride march took place 50 years ago, on 1 July 1972. What began as one event in London has since grown into more than 160 Pride events across the UK – from big cities to small towns. Pride has also spread to more than 100 countries, making it one of the most ubiquitous and successful global movements of all time.

How did it all begin?

After the Stonewall uprising in New York in 1969 – when the patrons of gay bars fought back against police harassment – the newly formed gay liberation movement in the USA decided to organise protests to coincide with the anniversary. The idea spread to the UK, and a group of us in the Gay Liberation Front in London came up with the idea of holding a celebratory and defiant "Gay Pride" march, to challenge queer invisibility and the prevailing view that we should be ashamed of our homosexuality. The ethos of Pride was born.

This was an era of de facto censorship of LGBT+ issues. There was no media coverage of homophobic persecution, no public figures were openly LGBT+ and there were no positive representations of queer people. The only time we appeared in the press was when a gay person was arrested by the police, murdered by queer-bashers, outed by the tabloids, or exposed as a spy, child molester or serial killer.

This is why a Pride march was necessary: to show that we were proud of who we were. But a march was a gamble. Would anyone join us?

Back then, most LGBTs were closeted and dared not reveal themselves publicly, fearing police victimisation. Many aspects of same-sex behaviour were still a crime, given that homosexuality had been only partially decriminalised in 1967. Some were afraid that coming out publicly would result in them being queer-bashed, rejected by family and friends or sacked by homophobic employers.

But, much to our surprise and delight, about 700 people turned out for the first UK Pride in 1972. It was a joyful, carnival-style parade through the streets of London, from Trafalgar Square via Oxford Street to Hyde Park.

We had a political message: LGBT+ liberation. Our banners proclaimed: "Gay is good" and "Gay is angry". Despite heavy policing and abuse from some members of the public, we made our point.

Buoyed by this first modest success, we had the confidence to organise further Pride marches in the years that followed. They had explicit political demands such as an equal age of consent, an end to police harassment and opposition to lesbian mothers losing custody of their children on the grounds that they were deemed to be unfit parents.

For most of the 1970s, Pride remained feisty but tiny, with fewer than 3,000 people. However, by the mid-1980s the numbers marching rose to 12,000.

Then we were hit with a triple whammy. First came the moral panic of the Aids pandemic. Dubbed the "gay plague", it demonised gay and bisexual men as the harbingers of death and destruction. Next the prime minister, Margaret Thatcher, attacked the right to be gay at the 1987 Conservative Party conference. And then, in 1988, Section 28 became law, prohibiting the so-called

PICTURED: Peter Tatchell in 1974 (above); Photos from the first ever Pride in London, 1972 (left, right and overleaf)

"promotion" of homosexuality by local authorities – the first new homophobic law in Britain for a century.

The LGBT+ community felt under attack – and we were. It brought us together and mobilised a fightback which was reflected in the turnout for Pride in 1988, with 30,000 marchers compared with 15,000 the year before. The march was angry and political, with some people attempting to storm Downing Street.

From 1988, Pride grew exponentially year on year. By 1997, there were 100,000 people on the march and the post-march festival on Clapham Common was attended by 300,000 revellers. This was the high point of Pride, run by – and for – the community, with strong LGBT+ human rights demands.

Since then, it has been downhill. A takeover by gay businesspeople at the turn of the century rebranded Pride as a "Mardi Gras" party and started charging for the post-march festival. Many people felt that Pride had been hijacked by commercial interests. Numbers plummeted, income crashed and the business consortium walked away.

For the past decade, the event has been run by a private community interest company, Pride in London, under contract and with funding from the mayor of London. It has been accused of being not representative of, or accountable to, the LGBT+ community, and of turning Pride into a depoliticised, overly commercial jamboree.

While some business sponsorship may be necessary to finance Pride, there is unease at the pre-eminence of commercial branding and advertising and the way huge extravagant corporate floats dominate the parade, overshadowing LGBT+ community groups.

Critics also question the participation of the police, arms manufacturers, fossil fuel companies, the Home Office and airlines involved in the deportation of LGBT+ refugees. Is this compatible with the liberation goals that inspired the first Pride? →

Back then, most LGBTs were closeted and dared not reveal themselves publicly, fearing police victimisation

→ And there is huge resentment that only 30,000 people are allowed to march in the parade, making Pride in London one of the smallest Prides of any Western capital city. Every year, thousands of people who want to march are turned away. This is against the original premise of Pride: that it should be open to everyone who wants to participate.

Pride in London claims that 1.5 million people attend. But there is no evidence to back this claim and it looks like hype to lure advertisers and sponsors. Even if we generously assume that 100,000 spectators line the route and there are 30,000 people in Trafalgar Square and 50,000 in Soho, plus 30,000 marchers, that's still only 210,000.

Discontent led to last year's Reclaim Pride march. It reverted to the roots of Pride, with a grassroots community focus, no corporate sponsors, and demands to ban LGBT+ conversion

As radical and committed as ever, we pioneers of Pride continue the liberation struggle we began half a century ago

therapy, reform the Gender Recognition Act and provide a safe haven for LGBT+ refugees fleeing persecution abroad – political issues that have been absent from the official Pride for two decades.

It cost only £1,800 to organise, refuting Pride in London's claims that Pride cannot exist without corporate funding to the tune of hundreds of thousands of pounds.

This year's Pride in London parade is on 2 July. The day before, on the 50th anniversary of the UK's first Pride, a handful of surviving Gay Liberation Front and 1972 Pride veterans will retrace the original route from Trafalgar Square to Hyde Park.

Among other things, we'll be urging the decriminalisation of LGBT+ people worldwide – including in the Commonwealth, where 35 out of the 54 member states still criminalise same-sex relations.

As radical and committed as ever, we pioneers of Pride continue the liberation struggle we began half a century ago. There will be no stopping until homophobia, biphobia and transphobia are history. ✖

Peter Tatchell is director of human rights organisation the Peter Tatchell Foundation

51(02):14/16|DOI:10.1177/03064220221110706

India's meaty issue

A ban on the sale of meat in some Indian states during a Hindu religious festival has made it dangerous to even admit to eating animals, reports **AISHWARYA JAGANI**

FOOD, AND THE history and culture associated with it, has always been fraught with political tension and ramifications far beyond what it really just is: sustenance. This is particularly true of India and South Asia, where vegetarians and meat eaters are often divided by religion, caste and class - leading to clashes, and sometimes violence, between vegetarians and meat-eaters, or 'non-vegetarians', as they are called in India. The uniquely Indian term 'non-vegetarian' is a nod to how vegetarianism is promoted as the norm and standard in the country.

This conceals the fact that only about 44% of Indians are vegetarian. But in India, vegetarianism isn't just a choice, it is often a marker of caste, class and religion. Signs advertising apartments to rent only to vegetarians, or 'pure-veg' restaurants marked by a green dot, aren't an unusual sign in the country. But food is increasingly being used as a tool of political domination against India's largest religious minority, Muslims.

On 4 April, the second day of Chaitra Navratri, a nine-day long Hindu festival, during which many Hindus fast or abstain from consuming meat, the mayor of a municipal corporation in Delhi called for a ban on the sale of raw meat, for the length of the festival.

The mayor, Mukkesh Surayan, claimed that "[Hindus'] religious beliefs and sentiments are affected when they come across meat shops or when they have to bear with the foul smell on their way to offer prayers".

The move was met with widespread outrage and condemned as a gross violation of many constitutional rights,

and a targeted attack on the Muslim community.

Journalist, author and associate editor at The Hindu, Ziya Us Salam said that the Bharatiya Janata Party (BJP) government is trying to control the food habits of people, adding that the move sends out the message that "Navratri is paramount; Ramzan is subservient".

Food writer and author Krish Ashok said that a ban on the sale of meat during a festival is almost always a "political, religious and majoritarianism assertion – a way of putting a particular community in their place, if you will."

Over the last few years, with a shift towards right wing sentiment, the Muslim community in India has found itself the subject of multiple attacks - including calls for genocide, riots, police brutality, and controversies over Islamic practices like the hijab and halal meat.

"In this particular part of India [Delhi], small-scale meat sellers largely tend to be Muslims. It seems to be clearly targeted [at Muslims] – I don't think there is any doubt about that," Ashok added.

'If majoritarianism is good enough for Delhi...'
The move to temporarily ban the sale of meat in India's capital was welcomed by many radical groups, and members of India's ruling party BJP rushed to justify it. "If other communities respect the Hindu festival and welcome the decision, we will also show respect when their festivals will be celebrated [sic]," Parvesh Verma, a Delhi MP from the BJP party, told a leading news publication.

What Verma failed to take into consideration was that the Muslim

festival of Ramadan was also underway, and meat is a large part of *iftar* (the evening meal) celebrations. He also failed to consider that in many Indian states, including West Bengal, Odisha, Bihar and Jharkhand, fish and meat are part of the religious offerings made during festivals.

Neetu Mattas, who is part of a Hindu (Pandit) community from Kashmir, shared how offering meat to certain deities on the ninth day of Navratri is an important ritual in her community, one that is still followed today. "The Navratri ban is unfair and unfortunate as it violates every Indian's fundamental right of choice," she added.

Moreover, the meat ban is bound to hit small businesses the worst.

This directive to ban the sale of meat did not extend to larger meat delivery businesses such as Licious, FreshToHome or Meatigo, but it forced small butcher shops, usually run by Muslims, to shut down for days on end - causing a significant loss of revenue. Historian and food writer Rana Safvi pointed out in a tweet how the meat ban will hit underprivileged Muslims the most, as they cannot afford to shop at online meat delivery companies like Licious. They depend on neighbourhood meat shops for *iftar* requirements, she tweeted.

This move to ban meat comes on the heels of a controversy over Indian Muslim students wearing the hijab, a head-covering, in Karnataka schools, and protests against the sale of halal, which refers to the Islamic practice of humanely slaughtering an animal for consumption. ➔

 People being lynched on suspicion of cow slaughter has increased

Every Muslim understands what this 'ban' means, but we can't even express our anger

→ This persecution of Muslims in India tends to spring from a fear of supposed affronts to Hinduism, fanned by the ruling party of India. '*Hindu khatre mein hai*' meaning 'Hindus are in danger' is a common refrain popularised by the BJP that sums up how many (but not all) Hindus in India feel.

"In how they feel, Hindus under Hindutva are in danger of becoming a majority with a minority complex, plagued by a sense of paranoia and persecution," historian Ramchandra Guha said in a Scroll op-ed.

"However, in how they act, Hindus under Hindutva are in danger of becoming a majority with a majority complex," he added.

Hindutva is a radical ideology that seeks to establish the hegemony of Hindus and Hinduism in India.

Former Chief Minister of Jammu and Kashmir, Omar Abdullah tweeted against the meat ban, saying, "During Ramzan we don't eat between sunrise and sunset. I suppose it's OK if we ban every non-Muslim resident or tourist from eating in public, especially in the Muslim dominated areas. If majoritarianism is right for South Delhi, it has to be right for J&K [Jammu and Kashmir]."

The weaponisation of vegetarianism

The political battle over meat has always been a point of contention, with the consumption of beef or cow meat (a creature considered sacred by many Hindus) at the heart of the issue.

Cow slaughter is prohibited to some degree in close to 20 of India's 28 states – but the weaponisation of cow protection and vegetarianism has intensified only since 2014, when the BJP came into power.

Since 2014, instances of people (usually Muslims or those from marginalised castes) being lynched to death on suspicion of cow slaughter have increased exponentially. "97% of lynching instances in the country [from 2010 to 2017] have taken place after 2014, according to Home Ministry figures. That says it all," said Salam.

Many upscale restaurants in India resort to using euphemisms such as "buff" or "meat" instead of "beef", even though they serve water buffalo meat, which is perfectly legal in India.

While one in 13 Indians admit to consuming meat (15% of whom are Hindu), according to the NSSO (National Sample Survey Office), the prevalence of right-wing Hindutva sentiment in the country has forced many people to keep quiet about their beef consumption.

Unconstitutional and illegal

Mayor Suryaan's order was followed by an "appeal" by the East Delhi Municipal Corporation, to shut down meat shops. Neither order was legally valid, since a mayor does not have the power to enforce such a ban. The statements also violated Indians' fundamental rights to freedom of trade, equality, life and personal liberty, and went against multiple Supreme Court and High Court judgements that have upheld the right to autonomy over food.

Although there was no official directive banning the sale of meat, butcher shops in Delhi remained shut out of fear of action by the authorities, or violence by Hindu vigilante groups.

"Owners decided to keep shops closed as the mayor has threatened serious actions against them," Sanjay Kumar, manager at Bombay Fish Shop, told the New India Express.

"Every Muslim understands what this 'ban' means, but we can't even express our anger. They are now using our religion to attack the bread we eat," Mehfooz Alam, a 65-year old butcher

ABOVE: A woman praying to a cow in Beawar, India. Slaughtering cows is prohibited to some extent in 20 of the 28 Indian states, with cows considered sacred in Hinduism

who works in Delhi's INA market, told Indian rights organisation Article14.

Index approached other meat sellers in Delhi, but they were reluctant to comment on the ban, claiming that

they had always shut down their shops during Navratri. It's unclear if this is true, or if they were too afraid to speak to a journalist.

"As much as we would like to believe that food unites, the truth is that food actually divides," said Ashok.

Ashok said that we as a society need to reflect on the notion of attaching purity labels to food. "We wouldn't have the kind of violence that we see today - [with vigilante groups] beating up people, lynching people - if there was no concept of purity attached to what you eat," he said. "Today a Muslim feels insecure when he runs a *dhaba* (a small eatery); a Muslim feels insecure ferrying cattle; a Muslim feels insecure offering prayers; a Muslim woman feels insecure while wearing hijab," said Salam.

"What is important today is the right to life, and the right to livelihood of Muslims is being encroached upon. And the institutions of government, and our state are silent bystanders," he added. ✖

Aishwarya Jagani is a freelance journalist based in India

51(02):17/19|DOI:10.1177/03064220221110710

Jennings

Our cartoonist turns his attention to the pre-historic perils of speaking truth to power

51(02):20/21|DOI:10.1177/03064220221110711

BEN JENNINGS:
an award-winning
cartoonist for The
Guardian and The
Economist whose
work has been
exhibited around
the world

My three years of hell in an Uyghur 're-education' camp

GULBAHAR HAITIWAJI is one of just a few who has dared to speak out about China's attempts to break and brainwash her and millions of her fellow Uyghurs. We share an extract of her survivor's story, with an introduction by **RAHIMA MAHMUT**

GULBAHAR HAITIWAJI'S BOOK How I Survived a Chinese Re-education Camp, written with Le Figaro journalist Rozenn Morgat, is much more than just one person's story. It is a survivor testimony, a piece of evidence, a voice for the handful of survivors in exile and documentation of atrocity. And it is also a symbol of Gulbahar's bravery. When Gulbahar was released, she was warned by the same regime that had just brutalised her to never even whisper a word of what she had experienced. Instead, she went on to write an entire book.

Gulbahar is one of millions that have been held in concentration camps across the Uyghur homeland, but she is one of very few that have been able to escape. Gulbahar's daughter, Gulhumar, and husband, Kerim, relentlessly campaigned for her release. The French government even lobbied on her behalf. The success of these interventions demonstrates the impact foreign governments can have. World leaders should take note; each time a Uyghur is detained or deported whilst the international community does nothing, an active choice has been made not to protect human life.

As I was reading Gulbahar's story, I was struck by how much it echoes those of other prisoners from China's past. Five years ago, I translated a prison memoir called The Land Drenched in Tears by the Tatar woman Söyüngül Chanisheff. For the four years that I spent translating this book, I felt that I was living inside Söyüngül's mind. The strength and faith she carried with her changed the way I saw the world.

Söyüngül was imprisoned during the Cultural Revolution (1966-76) and the indoctrination and violence she faced are mirrored in Gulbahar's experiences. In Söyüngül's own words, she feels lucky to have been interned before the age of high-tech terror. In her memoir, rare moments of relief come when Söyüngül describes the community that existed in the prison camp; the discussions, even arguments, that would break out between the imprisoned women. There is no space for this shred of normality in the camps now; 24-hour high-tech surveillance means that detainees are forced to endure the violence packed together in tiny cells, in silence. This is a kind of torture in itself. →

ABOVE: Rahima Mahmut at a protest in London's Chinatown

We are haunted by our memories of being watched

→ During the Cultural Revolution, the Chinese Communist Party refined their methods of brutality and erasure, including the forced labour, state violence and cultural destruction that continue today. But now they have developed a new machinery of control – the surveillance equipment that is used throughout the concentration camps, and the wider region. Gulbahar often speaks of camp survivors being broken by their trauma – becoming "shadows" whose "souls are dead". In doing so, she puts poetic description to the impact of this constant surveillance. This is true for survivors, but also for all of us in the diaspora, who live in a state of lingering psychological distress. We are haunted by our memories of being watched and it seeps into who we are.

But the Chinese government's attempts to weave surveillance into Gulbahar's existence have failed. Instead, she has found the strength to break the patterns of silence that have sustained the repression of our people for so long. Far from sitting with her pain in fear, Gulbahar has been touring, giving speeches, doing press interviews. She is making sure the world remembers there are others, like Nadira, that we still need to save. Gulbahar carries that responsibility with her, and she takes personal risks to seek justice for those she left behind. The least the rest of us can do is speak up for them too. ✖

Rahima Mahmut is UK director of the World Uyghur Congress

How I Survived a Chinese 'Re-education' Camp

Gulbahar Haitiwaji

"RIGHT ! LEFT! At ease!" There were 40 of us in the room, all women, wearing blue pyjamas. It was a nondescript rectangular classroom, no more than 50m2 (500 square feet). A big metal shutter, perforated with tiny holes that let the light in, hid the outside world from us. Eleven hours a day, the world was reduced to this room. Our slippers squeaked on linoleum as two Han soldiers relentlessly kept time. This was called 'physical education.' In reality, it was tantamount to military training. Our exhausted bodies moved through the space in unison, back and forth, side to side, corner to corner. When the soldier bellowed 'At ease!' in Mandarin, our regiment of prisoners froze. He would then order us to remain still. This could last half an hour, or just as often a whole hour, or even several. When it did, our legs would begin to prickle all over with pins and needles. Our bodies, still warm and restless, struggled not to sway in the moist heat. We could smell our own foul breath. We panted like oxen. sometimes, one or another of us would faint. If she failed to come to on her own, a guard would yank her to her feet and slap her awake. If she collapsed again, he would drag her out of the room, and we'd never see her again. Ever. At first, I found this shocking. Before long, it was just business as usual.

I'd been here for three days now. When I wasn't on the verge of tears, I sometimes stifled a giggle over what a ridiculous spectacle it was: the two men in their martial tones choreographing us, 40 little ersatz soldiers. We stood in impeccable ranks facing a portrait of Xi Jinping, moon face and paternalistic smile against an azure blue background. You'd think we were in Tiananmen Square. Stuck in his frame, he watched us march back and forth across the room, hands obediently folded behind our backs, like in the annual military parades. I wanted to scream in his face that I'd remain a free woman for the rest of my life, that his system would never break me.

Three days I'd been here. They'd told us training would last for two weeks. After that the theory classes would begin. I didn't know how I was going to hold out. How had I not broken

 ## Our exhausted bodies moved through the space in unison

down already? This was Baijiantan. That was all the information I'd managed to glean after leaving the jail, from a sign stuck in a dried-out ditch where a few empty plastic bags drifted about. Baijiantan was on the outskirts of Karamay, a no-man's-land from which three buildings rose, each the size of a small airport. Beyond the barbed-wire fence, there was nothing but desert as far as the eye could see.

Among the 40 new arrivals were petite older women stooping in the thick cloth of their blue pyjamas, wilting teens lost in the billows of the same, and women like me, hunched over from exhaustion and sleepless nights on a straw mattress. Nadira was one of these, too. There she stood, perfectly erect in the row of women facing me. She was the only person I really made a connection with. I met her the first day. When the female guards opened the door to my 'room,' she was waiting there alone, in the middle of the dormitory with its row of numbered wooden planks: our beds. Nadira was in Bunk No. 8. I was assigned Bunk No. 9. That coincidence was enough to draw us together. My arrival had made her feel better; she'd been there for several hours. One of the first things she asked was: 'Why do you smell so good?' I told her about the bra I'd recovered from the locker at the jail. We had a good laugh. Her sparkling eyes inspired confidence. For once, I wasn't suspicious. 'We can share it, if you want,' I said. 'The bra, I mean. I'll just set it between our beds at night, and that way we can both smell it.' She liked that idea. 'Oh, you'd do that? That's so nice, Gulbahar! Thank you!'

In exchange for the wafts of Narciso Rodriguez, she showed me around the dormitory, which still reeked dizzyingly of fresh paint: the bucket for doing your business, which she gave a wrathful kick; the window with its metal shutter always drawn tight; the two cameras panning back and forth in high corners of the rooms. That was it. No real mattress to speak of. No furniture. No toilet paper. No sheets. No sink. Just two of us in the gloom and the muffled bang of heavy cell doors slamming shut.

That first day Nadira did a lot of talking. She paced around the room like a caged tiger, hurling

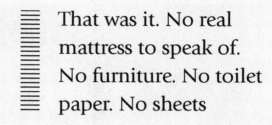

That was it. No real mattress to speak of. No furniture. No toilet paper. No sheets

scraps of her story at the walls. She had been a TV host on a cultural channel in Karamay. A 'terrific show broadcast in the Uyghur language, a nice way to spend the evening,' she added as I looked on, flabbergasted. She'd wanted to become a professional dancer, do opening ceremonies for political officials in Xinjiang. That hadn't panned out but TV was a respectable consolation prize. You were still on a stage with the spotlights, the energy of a live audience. Besides, Nadira had a special look to her - the kind of beauty that the 'lights took a shine to,' as she put it. It was her thing. She lived with her husband and children in a pretty house downtown. One day, plainclothes agents had showed up at her door. 'Did you know that prayer is forbidden?' they asked. 'I don't know how they found out. Sure, I prayed every now and then,' she whispered as if the cameras could hear us (and maybe they could). They hadn't said where they were taking her. All she'd heard was the same word I had: 'school.' Next thing she knew, she'd found herself in Baijiantan. I realised that this was no school. It was a 're-education' camp.

* * *

We were also taught patriotic songs while standing in formation. `You must learn them by heart, or you will be punished.' All day long, we croaked out these refrains. Since Nadira had a pretty voice, the two soldiers had given her a special task. At their command, she would step forward from the ranks and go stand beside them. Lifting her right hand, she would launch into the national anthem and, on her signal, the rest of our voices, husky from being silenced too often, rose in the classroom: 'Stand up! Stand up! Stand up! We ➔

ABOVE: Gulbahar Haitiwaji is a refugee who survived the infamous 're-education' camps in China. Here, she attends the World Uyghur Congress, in Prague, in November 2021

→ are billions of one heart, braving the enemies' fire. March on! Braving the enemies' fire, march on! March on! March on! On!' It was ridiculous.

In Cell 202, we had been left to our own devices. Idleness, our daily burden, stripped away our ability to think. Tedium alone, across drawn-out stretches of time, occupied our minds. For whole days at a time, we were dying of boredom. Oh my God, we were bored! Round and round in circles we'd go when all we wanted was to leave, run away, scream.

Here, the military rules were designed to break us. Sheer physical fatigue robbed us of the

desire to speak. Our days were punctuated by the screech of whistles: on waking, at mealtime, at bedtime. Lunches and dinners followed one after another, during which we were not allowed to speak. The guards always had an eye on us. If one of us whispered or wiped her mouth, she was accused of praying. If one of us turned down her food, she was called an 'Islamist terrorist' and ordered to polish off her plate. The wardens claimed our food was halal. We had no choice but to eat it. At night, I would collapse on my bunk in a stupor. I had lost all sense of time. There was no clock. I guessed at the hour of day from how cold or hot it felt. I lived in terror of the guards.

We hadn't seen daylight since we arrived. All the windows were blocked by those metal shutters. Left to my own devices, I debated with

If one of us whispered or wiped her mouth, she was accused of praying

I didn't want to start crying in front of the camera

myself. But what was the point of wasting what little energy I had left? We were surrounded by desert as far as the eye could see. Rahmanjan had promised I'd be given a phone, but none had materialised. Apart from him, who else even knew I was being held here? Had my sister been notified, or Aynur, Kerim and Gulhumar? It was a waking nightmare. I couldn't even open up to my fellow detainees because the cameras were always watching. I was tired, so tired. I couldn't even think anymore.

Naptime was my salvation. After lunch, the guards would lead us back to our cells, where we were allowed to lie down on our straw mattresses for about half an hour. Some of my fellow detainees took the chance to doze off; others stayed awake and whispered. For me, that time was a retreat into my secret garden. No one could keep me from going there. It was inside my head. Every day, to the soothing sound of Nadira's regular breathing, I cultivated happy memories. They reminded me where I was from. Thanks to them, I managed not to be completely overwhelmed.

Half-asleep, I picked up the train of my thoughts where I'd left off the night before. Barcelona, Fontainebleau, the gardens at Giverny, the little towns in the Yvelines we'd drive through on Sundays, the trunk of our car full of fruits, vegetables, and flowers from La Ferme de Viltain. I cared for these memories lovingly in order of preference, sorting them chronologically, bringing them back to life with countless details. 'What are you thinking about?' Nadira would often murmur, her voice thick. Tears would spring to my eyes. My throat tightened. I didn't want to start crying in front of the camera. Instead, I stared at the white ceiling. 'Nothing,' I said. 'Nothing.'

Baijiantan is a massive labyrinth. A handful of guards would escort us to each of our activities in groups, by dormitory. Once naptime was over,

even a moment's privacy was impossible.

To reach the bathrooms, classrooms, or mess hall required navigating a series of endless fluorescent-lit hallways. At their far ends, automatic security doors sealed off the maze-like airlocks. One thing was for sure: all this had just sprung up from the ground. Everything here was new. The reek of paint from the spotless walls was a ubiquitous reminder of that fact.

It seemed like the premises of a factory, but I didn't yet have a handle on just how big it was. In Baijiantan, daily life came down to a triangular ambit: cell - classroom - mess hall. Only the sheer number of prisoners and guards whose paths we crossed when being herded around in a group gave me an inkling of just how enormous the camp really was. Every day, I saw new faces, zombie-like, bags under the eyes. So far, I had never seen the same group of prisoners twice. The first day, Nadira and I had been the only ones in our cell. By that night, there were seven of us. Now there were twelve.

A little quick maths: I'd counted 16 cells, including mine, each with twelve bunks, twelve prisoners crammed in on top of each other. Multiply the number of cells by the number of prisoners, and that made for almost 200 detainees at Baijiantan. Two hundred women torn from their families. Two hundred lives locked up until further notice. And the camp just kept getting ever fuller before our very eyes.

You could tell the new arrivals from their distraught faces. They still tried to meet your gaze in the hallway. The ones who'd been there for longer looked down at their feet. They shuffled around in close ranks, like robots. They snapped to attention without batting an eye, whenever a whistle ordered them to. Good God, what had been done to make them that way? I shuddered at the thought of finding out. ✖

This is an extract from How I Survived a Chinese 'Re-education' Camp (Canbury Press) by Gulbahar Haitiwaji and Rozenn Morgat. Index readers can get a 20% discount on this new book (see p.72)

51(02):22/27|DOI:10.1177/03064220221110717

One step ahead of the game

Local TV in China is full of stories exposing government corruption. But, as **DAN CHEN** writes, it's a sly way to entrench state power

THROUGHOUT THE COVID-19 pandemic many Chinese people have endured especially stringent controls over their movement and livelihoods, as evidenced by the recent lockdowns in Shanghai. Despite this, Chinese people have strongly complied with these controls and have indicated strong trust in and support of the government. Although there is a prevailing view in the West that the Chinese people are victimised by their government, polling and research, including my own, show consistently high support within China for the government. How can this be?

While the answer is multifaceted, there is one particularly interesting

LEFT: A cameraman in Yunnan province, China. According to one survey, a greater percentage of the Chinese population trust television compared to newspapers

My research found that many local leaders serve their political goals by using the local media as a watchdog of street-level bureaucrats. As a result of such reporting, citizen grievances tend to get resolved quickly. Thus, while the initial media reporting is critical, the resolution of each issue becomes a positive news story that signals the effectiveness of the Chinese system. For local politicians, a savvy and effective media strategy can be a critical factor in shaping public opinion and advancing their careers.

Public opinion has become a prominent factor in Chinese politics and governance in the reform era. In 1987, the Party General Secretary's report to the 13th Party Congress formalised the policy of "supervision by public opinion". Under this policy, certain media outlets were extended a precarious leash into critical news reporting, and some were successful at achieving implicit political approval. Scholars have interpreted this as serving the central government's interests by collecting information on emerging problems, holding local officials accountable and diverting citizen blame from the central leadership to local officials.

Within today's multifaceted and complex media landscape, my research reveals a similarly strategic use of criticism. I focused on television news because it reaches over 95% of the Chinese population with minimal rural-urban disparities. Television also enjoys a high level of credibility in China. According to the 2015 Asian Barometer Survey, 70% of the Chinese population trust television while 57% trust newspapers. I conducted fieldwork at 12 television stations between 2012 and 2018, comprising of one central-level station, three provincial-level stations

and eight municipal-level stations. I collected data using ethnographic observation, interviews, a survey and content analysis.

From this research I found that critical reporting is uniquely plentiful on local television stations at provincial and municipal levels. Aggrieved citizens can use television news programmes' hotlines to criticise, complain and demand change. This feature of Chinese local media has given rise to a unique brand of advocacy journalism.

In Jiangsu province, a popular local news programme called Zero Distance has repeatedly demonstrated its effectiveness at delivering popular television and governance outcomes.

On 23 February 2017, Zero Distance reported a news story about a misbehaving local official. According to an anonymous hotline call to the programme in November 2016, a civil affairs department director named Xu was repeatedly absent from his work at a street committee in a district of Nanjing, the capital city of Jiangsu. Reporters then started a three-month investigation by disguising as ordinary citizens in need of government help on pension funds, an issue of Director Xu's responsibility. When he was unavailable, the excuse from Xu's coworkers was that "Director Xu is in a meeting". Through meticulous investigation, reporters discovered that Xu had been playing mahjong at a nearby mahjong →

feature of China's media system that helps. The Chinese government is extraordinarily strict about controlling the media, but some local government leaders utilise critical reporting to address local issues.

The resolution of each issue becomes a positive news story that signals the effectiveness of the Chinese system

→ room extensively during work hours. In the next day's broadcast, Zero Distance aired a follow-up report stating that the street committee had put Xu on immediate leave and under investigation by the discipline commission of the district. That same day, the street committee convened an organisation-wide meeting to educate its officials about their duties and disciplines.

The televised criticism of local officials contrasts with the taboo on criticism of central government officials, agencies and policies - a taboo that is enforced by brutal suppression.

It would be wrong, however, to view the local scene as a green shoot of media freedom. What I found is that some local leaders encourage the criticism to increase their capacity for bureaucratic control and advance their careers. The critical television programmes serve as the local bosses' eyes and ears, identifying underlings who are failing to provide good public service and keeping tabs on the public mood. Seen in this light, criticism that is allowed and even encouraged on local television should be understood as a result of political control, rather than a lack of it.

Still, the criticism gets results, at least some of the time. For example, on 19 March 2017, Zero Distance covered a story from a hotline call by a forklift driver, who claimed that he received an unusually expensive parking ticket that was issued illegally. After the initial broadcast of the case, more forklift drivers who received similar parking tickets came forward. A month later, the journalistic investigation revealed a scheme in the local district government to solicit bribes from forklift drivers. As a result of this reporting, the local district government apologised on television to the forklift drivers, returned the illegally charged parking fines, and thanked the journalists for their supervision of government work.

Recently, on 2 March 2022, a nightly news programme broadcast by Yangzhou municipal television

The critical television programmes serve as the local bosses' eyes and ears, identifying underlings who are failing to provide good public service

station in Jiangsu province reported a case of illegal law enforcement. A small business owner named Zhang called the programme's hotline to complain that a pile of construction waste was dumped at his storefront by the urban management bureau in the local township. Reporters found out that a few days earlier, officials from the town urban management bureau asked Zhang to pay overdue rent for his storefront, which is part of a government-owned building that had been mismanaged. Zhang has rented the same storefront for over 20 years and had always paid rent on time, but there had been nobody in charge of rent collection in the past two years prior to the urban management bureau officials suddenly showing up. Zhang requested that the officials provide documentation that they were authorised to collect his rent, but none was provided and Zhang refused to pay. Two of Zhang's neighbours encountered the same situation, but they decided to pay the overdue rent after rubbish was dumped at their storefront. During a phone interview with a reporter, a medium-level official from the urban management bureau explained that dumping rubbish was an idea from the "higher-up" and boasted about dumping trash as a much faster and more effective tactic than going through the legal and administrative channels. When the Yangzhou television station broadcasted the story, the programme's host was clearly critical of the town urban management bureau, referring to their rubbish-dumping tactic of law enforcement as "reckless" and "detrimental to their image".

The next day, 3 March 2022, a follow-up report was broadcast. The footage showed the dumped rubbish being cleared out with a voiceover stating that local government leaders had begun an investigation into illegal law enforcement. The vice mayor of the town went on television to promise that the local government would educate and discipline its officials to prevent similar incidents from happening in the future. The report ended with an interview with Zhang, who was satisfied with the outcome.

Instances such as these demonstrate how China's local governance is improved through these narrow openings for journalism and public criticism. By emphasising happy endings to public grievances, the follow-on news broadcasts work to deepen public approval for the government in general.

This feature of China's media system is demonstrating a successful method at disciplining street-level officials and improving governance. In this way, the government not only monopolises propaganda but also expropriates criticism. These findings expand our understanding of Chinese journalism from its suppression to its manipulation. Along the way, this media system invigorates a unique brand of advocacy journalism in cooperation with the government. ✖

Dan Chen is an assistant professor of political science at the University of Richmond and author of Convenient Criticism: Local Media and Governance in Urban China

51(02):28/30|DOI:10.1177/03064220221110740

Welcome to the Kingdom of Impunity

Journalists in Haiti face corruption, violence and even murder, which largely goes unpunished. **MICHAEL DEIBERT** shines a light on those who refuse to be silenced

JULY MARKS A year since the assassination of Haiti's president, Jovenel Moïse. Since then, the country has been deep in a political crisis, with armed gangs taking control and both murders and kidnappings widespread. The situation for journalism and freedom of speech in this tumultuous country remains fraught, where a cacophony of opinions often collide with the reality of powerful actors willing to defend their advantages with guns.

Two important milestones in the Caribbean nation have already passed this year: the centenary of author Jacques Stephen Alexis's birth and the 22nd anniversary of the murder of Jean Dominique, one of Haiti's most prominent journalists, an advocate for free speech and the owner of Radio Haiti Inter. Alongside Dominique, Jean-Claude Louissaint, the caretaker at the radio station, was also killed.

In 2014, nine people were accused of the killings, many of whom had links to former president Jean-Bertrand Aristide, although none have yet been tried. Before his death, Dominique said he had "no weapons other than my journalism, my microphone and my unquenchable faith as a militant for true change".

Dominique and Louissaint were killed in April 2000, in the midst of a bitterly-contested election campaign. The killings interrupted the fitful democratisation the country had witnessed since overthrowing the 29-year Duvalier family dictatorship in 1986. In the years since, although elections have occurred

with relative frequency in Haiti, the actual fact of democracy – transparent, uncontested ballots after which politicians act as effective advocates for their constituents – has not.

The two decades have seen the institutionalisation of violence against journalists and other critical voices in the country to such a degree that some refer to Haiti as "the kingdom of impunity".

This permissiveness somehow coexists with a noisy and rambunctious press corps along with an intellectual milieu that frequently serves up piercing commentary directed at the country's powerful.

Haiti has been ruled for the last decade by the Tèt Kale Party (PHTK),

a political group created by former singer Michel Martelly, who served as president from 2011 until 2016. High-ranking members of the party have been dogged by allegations of links to weapons-smuggling, drug-trafficking and illegal armed groups, and recent years have seen the party fight a ruthless pitched battle with its political opposition, which has also proven it has little aversion to bloodshed.

Since Moïse's assassination, the country has been ruled by an interim prime minister, Ariel Henry (who local human rights organisations accuse of possible links to the murder), in an uneasy coalition of some of Moïse's bitterest political enemies. Civil society, though vibrant, remains largely locked out of real political power.

"There is no justice today in Haiti, and the example of Jean Dominique is there to prove it 22 years later," said Kettly Mars, a poet and novelist. →

BELOW: Hundreds of Haitian journalists march to the Justice Hall in Port-au-Prince, Haiti, in April 2000. The journalists demanded freedom of the press and justice for journalist Jean Dominique who was assassinated two weeks earlier

LEFT: Photojournalist Dieu Nalio Chery was injured covering protests outside parliament in Haiti's capital Port-au-Prince, September 2019

"We live in disorganised, anarchic and dangerous dictatorships, supported and tolerated by an international community whose motivations are not well understood. Healthy voices and the critical mass that could affect change cannot yet rise because the system is weighed down by reactionaries who take advantage of this chaotic situation. The balance of power is in great favour of the status quo."

The impulse towards free speech and creative expression has a long and politically-charged history in Haiti.

During the country's "Revolution of 1946", which marked the overthrow of authoritarian President Élie Lescot, the movement to oust him was spearheaded by young Marxist intellectuals in the capital.

They included Alexis and fellow author René Depestre, and the painter Gérald Bloncourt – a group that coalesced around a revolutionary weekly called La Ruche (The Beehive). The movement drew inspiration from a series of lectures that French surrealist André Breton gave in Port-au-Prince at the end of 1945, during which he spoke about personal freedom and railed against dictatorship.

During the long night of Duvalierism – encompassing the 1957-71 rule of François Duvalier (known as Papa Doc) and the 1971-86 rule of his son Jean-Claude (Baby Doc) – stations such as Radio Haiti Inter tried to push the envelope of what was acceptable under a capricious tyranny.

After being brutally attacked and the station shut down by Duvalier in November 1980, Dominique, its owner, fled into exile for several years along with his wife and co-director Michèle Montas. Meanwhile, station manager Richard Brisson took part in an ill-fated attempted invasion in the north of the country by Haitian exiles, and was executed in January 1982.

As the movement to oust the Duvalier dictatorship gathered steam in the 1980s, musicians including Manno Charlemagne supplied a soundtrack of pointed political critique in songs such as *Ayiti pa Forè* (Haiti Is Not a Forest), which pointedly asked: "If Haiti is not a forest, why are there so many beasts around?"

The military juntas of the 1990s were greeted with expressions of popular discontent such as the song *Ké M Pa Sote* (My Heart Doesn't Leap) from the band Boukman Eksperyans.

Once democratic icon Aristide's drift towards despotism in the early 2000s was addressed obliquely in works such as Gary Victor's novel *À L'angle des Rues Parallèles* and the filmmaker Raoul Peck's Moloch Tropical, as well as more directly in works such as film director Arnold Antonin's GNB Kont Attila.

But over the last 20 years, there has been a staccato litany of killings of those who dared inform the public. In July 2005, the poet and journalist Jacques Roche was kidnapped and slain in Port-au-Prince. Two years later, photojournalist Jean-Rémy Badio was gunned down outside his home.

In March 2012, Jean Liphète Nelson, the founder of Radio Boukman in the impoverished neighbourhood of Cité Soleil, was killed by heavy gunfire. Both Pétion Rospide, of Radio Sans Fin, and Néhémie Joseph, of Radio Mega, were killed in 2019, with Joseph having publicly shared his fears over death threats from PHTK politicians.

Only a few days before Moïse's →

 We face death on a daily basis. When we leave home, there is no certainty that we will return

Haitian justice is struggling to deliver justice. The launch of the investigations for all the crimes are flawed

→ assassination last summer, Radio Vision 2000 reporter Diego Charles and feminist activist Antoinette Duclaire were slain in Port-au-Prince's Christ-Roi neighbourhood. Just months before, Duclaire told the television programme Haiti Sa Kap Kwit: "We face death on a daily basis. When we leave home, there is no certainty that we will return."

More recently, in January this year, journalists Wilguens Louissaint and Amady John Wesley were killed by gang members as they attempted to report on a gang incursion in the mountainous Port-au-Prince suburb of Laboule. Journalists are also frequently mistreated by security forces when covering demonstrations.

"Unfortunately, crimes against journalists have all gone unpunished," said Frantz Duval, editor in chief of the daily newspaper Le Nouvelliste.

"This was the case during the time of the Duvalier dictatorship, and it is still the case since democratisation. Haitian justice is struggling to deliver justice. The launch of the investigations for all the crimes are flawed. Trials are impossible in the majority of cases, [but] freedom of the press is still alive in Haiti. There have never been so many journalists, journalism schools, media of all kinds. Speech is free and even totally unbridled. The powers-that-be hope the cacophony will shield them from an effective press [but] the number [of journalists] does not equal quality and self-censorship does the rest."

Those who criticise power in Haiti often find themselves drawing the attention of the baz, as the armed groups in the country's more impoverished quarters are known. These gangs, often made up of young men and boys, act as neighbourhood protectors, tax collectors, muscle for political interests and freelance criminals. The use of these armed gangs as a political tool first came to prominence with partisans of former president Aristide's party in the late 1990s and early 2000s, but has since spread throughout the country.

The baz come with unbridled power and protection from political connections. In November 2018, after a group of gunmen raided the capital's La Saline slum in an attack the UN said left at least 26 people dead, three of those allegedly involved in the attack were sanctioned by the US State Department for their alleged roles in the killings – former police officer Jimmy "Barbecue" Chérizier and two Moïse government officials.

Chérizier subsequently announced the formation of the G9 An Fanmi E Alye, an alliance of armed groups around Port-au-Prince.

Perhaps the most chilling event for local free speech advocates was the March 2018 disappearance of journalist Vladimir Legagneur in the neighbourhood of Grand Ravine, a gang-ridden district in the south of Port-au-Prince.

Another of those who has felt the sharp end of Haiti's political wars is Dieu Nalio Chery, an award-winning photographer who worked for the Associated Press in Haiti for several years. He fled after being targeted by threats from armed groups last year.

"It's been very hard to work as a journalist for the last five years with the growth of gangs everywhere in Haiti, especially in the capital," he said. In September 2019, Chery was shot (apparently by accident) by a sitting senator, PHTK's Jean Marie Ralph Féthière, as he attempted to cover clashes between protesters and legislators outside parliament.

"Journalists do not feel safe writing meaningful stories about gangs, kidnappings, and corruption, because gangs threaten them and there is a lack of access to information," Chery explained. "And local journalists face police brutality during protests because the police don't like them reporting their brutality against protesters."

The imbalance of power brought about by the hard grain of impunity in Haiti is something that also impacts those who work in the creative arts.

"Someone who has power and money in Haiti, he can prevent you from expressing yourself," said Jean D'Amérique, a poet, playwright and novelist whose books, such as last year's Soleil à Coudre, paint a piercing picture of modern Haiti.

"They will have no fear of doing so because they know that they do not necessarily have to answer to justice. We have all come to know it. If we speak or act until we concretely disturb those who want to take advantage of the privileges of power, we will be repressed."

This year marks the 61st anniversary of Jacques Stephen Alexis's death.

In April 1961, he led a small party of would-be rebels to land on the Haitian coast near Môle-Saint-Nicolas, a picturesque village in the north-west of the country still dotted with the ruins of French, Spanish and British forts. Hoping to topple the Duvalier dictatorship, Alexis and his compatriots were discovered and betrayed, and he was killed by the same forces he had critiqued in his work so eloquently years before. Years after his death, his name, like that of Jean Dominique, lives on in the hearts of many Haitians who believe that the country can – and must – change. ✖

Michael Deibert is an author, journalist, and researcher at Centro de Estudos Internacionais at Instituto Universitário de Lisboa

51(02):31/34|DOI:10.1177/03064220221110750

Politically corrected?

As Kenyans approach a general election in August, a list of words has been banned. **ISSA SIKITI DA SILVA** investigates why

AHEAD OF THE country's general election, Kenya's National Cohesion and Integration Commission (NCIC) has banned more than 20 words it said were inciting hatred, discrimination and violence against ethnic groups. The outrage the decision triggered will likely linger for many years to come.

In a country where politics has been infested by ethnic divisions since its independence from Britain, the state-controlled NCIC's decision has turned into a tribal war of words, as August's election draws near and the campaign heats up.

The list of illegal language includes the Swahili *madoadoa* (spots), *watu wa kurusha mawe* (those who throw stones) and *watajua hawajui* (they won't know what hit them).

There are also phrases in Sheng (Swahili pidgin), including *kama noma, noma, kama mbaya, mbaya*, which means "no matter what".

Kikuyu language featuring on the censor's checklist include *kihii* (young boy) and *uthamaki ni witu* (the throne is ours), alongside Kalenjin words such as *kimurkeldet* (brown teeth) and *otutu labotonik* (uproot the weed). Some English words have been banned too: fumigation, uncircumcised, eliminate and kill.

"This is a politically-motivated decision. We'll not accept it and we'll continue using these words no matter what happens," a man identified as Disco, who claims to be a William Ruto hard-line supporter, told Index on Censorship in Nairobi.

Ruto, the country's outgoing deputy president from the Kalenjin ethnic group, is the United Democratic Alliance flagbearer and one of the leading presidential contenders.

"We know who is behind this scandalous decision. It's Uhuru. When will these Kikuyu begin to understand that this country belongs to all Kenyans?" said another Ruto supporter nicknamed Roho, referring to the country's outgoing president Uhuru Kenyatta, a Kikuyu.

Kenya's first and third presidents, Jomo Kenyatta and Mwai Kibaki, were Kikuyu. Now, speculation is rife that opposition candidate Raila Odinga – chosen by Uhuru Kenyatta to succeed him ahead of Ruto – is about to appoint a Kikuyu woman, Martha Karua, as his running mate.

Some observers believe the NCIC included another alleged piece of hate speech on the list, *hatupangwingwi*, meaning "no one can manipulate us", because it seemed to target prominent families who have been in power for a long time, namely the Kikuyus and, particularly, the Kenyatta family.

The meaning is derived from Sipangwingwi, a hit song composed by popular rapper Exray, who claims his song is apolitical. *Hatupangwingwi* has since been adopted as a rally slogan by Ruto. Meanwhile, *kama noma, noma, kama mbaya, mbaya* can be found in the political language of Mombasa governor and Orange Democratic Movement deputy leader Hassan Ali Joho.

For Anna Gichuru, a Kikuyu vegetable trader, there is no doubt that the banned words and phrases are coded, and therefore dangerous. She hailed the NCIC for putting a stop to what she believed was a breeding ground for violence, intimidation, and chaos.

She says she still fails to understand why people from other ethnic groups hate the Kikuyu and blame them for everything that goes wrong in Kenya.

"We are peaceful people and mind our own business. We are all Kenyans and we shouldn't be fighting among ourselves on behalf of politicians who do nothing for us but enrich themselves and their families," she said.

NCIC chairman Samuel Kobia said that the commission had monitored Facebook, Twitter and YouTube, among others, and found that Facebook and Twitter were the main platforms where hate and incitement were spread through these banned words.

Gideon Chitanga, a political analyst from the Johannesburg-based Centre for the Study of Democracy, told Index that it was a governing responsibility to mitigate the negative and particularly violent use of language.

"In most cases where political violence is prevalent, before it gets physical, it starts with violent coding or targeting of certain individuals, then once they are coded in that way, the second thing that follows is physical violence," he said.

He explained that when the use of language was protected, it actually reinforced freedom of association.

"Those people who are potentially labelled are also undermined from exercising their freedom of association through intimidation and fear, thus the whole political system can be undermined through the use of violent and negative violent language." →

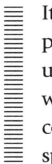

It is simply not possible that every use of a particular word would constitute hate speech

→ He called on the authorities to address the deeper structures or factors that feed into ethnic violence and the issue of derogatory language and warned governments not to regulate freedom of expression for fear of creating a slippery slope where the state can slowly encroach into civic rights.

Governments could end up adopting authoritarian practices, where they bracket anything that uses violent language. It could also infringe on artistic freedom, he explained.

"Commissions are normally set up through an act of parliament, and because of that it creates structures that sometimes allow governments to unfairly regulate broader civic freedoms," he said.

"This kind of work would require other civic bodies that will not only

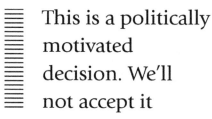

This is a politically motivated decision. We'll not accept it

identify these words and seek ways to deal with the perceived perpetrators, but also address other societal issues which are reflected through the use of such languages, part of it being political behaviour and deeply ingrained societal issues that feed into tribalism in Kenya."

Toby Mendel, executive director of the Centre for Law and Democracy, told Index that the ban certainly raised serious freedom of expression concerns.

"In general, while it is not only legitimate but also required under international law to ban a very narrow category of speech known as hate speech (as set out in Article 20(2) of the International Covenant on Civil and Political Rights), it must be noted that it

RIGHT: William Ruto, Kenya's deputy president and a presidential candidate in the upcoming elections, addresses a campaign rally in Nairobi in January

is simply not possible that every use of a particular word would constitute hate speech," he said.

He described the use of the extremely offensive N-word, which whilst sometimes used as hate speech does not always reach the extreme and narrow threshold of hate speech, even when used in racist terms.

"In some cases, the way it is used is not even racist and may even be used to highlight and push back on racism," he said, explaining how words such as this can also be used artistically or ironically.

"Banning the use of these words generally, even if only during an election period, is not legitimate," he said. "I would say that it is not even legitimate to ban outright their use by political parties and candidates, although this is obviously much narrower and hence less offensive to freedom of expression."

Mendel has suggested ways the commission could have approached the issue. One option would be bringing leading parties together to discuss a voluntary and reciprocal avoidance of certain words. Another is making clear that the use of these terms would be scrutinised carefully, with measures taken against usage constituting hate speech. Mendel said the NCIC could also have consulted with media outlets to see if it could reach an agreement either not to use these terms or to use them only when not in a racist context.

Successive attempts to get comments from the NCIC, the Media Council of Kenya and the Kenya Law Reform Commission failed, with some saying the issue was too sensitive to be commented on by foreign media. ✖

Issa Sikiti da Silva is an Index contributing editor based in West Africa

51(02):35/37|DOI:10.1177/03064220221110757

SPECIAL REPORT

"Anyone who believes that Ukraine should remain independent
and become part of Europe is already an enemy of Russia"

ANDREY KURKOV ON RUSSIA'S FEAR OF INDEPENDENT UKRAINIAN CULTURE AND ATTEMPTS TO CRUSH IT | CULTURE IN THE CROSS HAIRS, P.64

Losing battle for truth in Russian lecture halls

Being an academic in Russia has become too dangerous if you're on the side of truth, writes **ILYA MATVEEV**

OVER THE LAST decade I have been a professor at one of the best political science departments in Saint Petersburg – a beautiful, old, cultured city. I moved there from Moscow and never regretted it. But soon after Russia invaded Ukraine, I realised it was time to move again. And so I left, in haste, for Italy. I am now doing my last semester at the university that has become my home and I do not know when I will see Saint Petersburg – or Russia – again.

In the 1990s, political science – a non-existent discipline in the Soviet Union – was gradually institutionalised in Russian universities. Saint Petersburg in particular established several strong departments.

Since the early 2000s they have had to coexist with an authoritarian regime. For years, things have hung in a precarious balance. The European University at St Petersburg, arguably the best graduate school in social sciences in Russia, was shut down by the authorities twice – in 2008 and in 2017-2018. However, each time it reopened. Smolny College, a liberal arts institution affiliated with the old Saint Petersburg University, has been attacked by the university's most recent rector, an aggressive, unscrupulous Kremlin loyalist. Smolny had long maintained a close partnership with Bard College,

a beacon of liberal arts education in the United States. The authorities eventually declared Bard an "undesirable organisation" in Russia. Smolny had to cut all ties; after that, it was allowed to operate again.

In effect, social and political scientists in Saint Petersburg have been stuck between the normal and the emergency. The normal: intellectual excitement of research and the pleasure of working with colleagues. The emergency: preparing the department's office for a possible police search; signing a letter for the release of a jailed colleague; demanding the university's reopening at a street demonstration.

The regime's long shadow actually made teaching more meaningful. Despite everything, we were able and willing to tell our students the truth and we valued this opportunity while we still had it.

In authoritarian contexts, teaching paradoxically becomes a political act while still being fully compatible with Max Weber's dictum: "Politics is out of place in the lecture room." Weber differentiated between taking a stand and analysing political structures: for a professor, promoting specific political positions in the classroom would mean exercising undue influence on their students since the relationship between a professor and a student is asymmetrical. However, under constant pressure

from the authorities, a clear-eyed analysis in itself equals taking a stand. Classes on Russian politics (which I have taught for several years) are the most obvious example. The fact that Putin's regime is authoritarian is rather uncontroversial in political science. To discuss it with students means zooming in on its building blocks: control over political parties, elections, the media and significant parts of the economy. This, in turn, means creating a narrative that is in direct contradiction with government propaganda.

Of course, there are no facts independent from interpretation in social sciences. However, the two are not identical: facts do maintain relative autonomy, to use a Marxist term. Insisting on this autonomy is a political gesture in itself when the government engages in constant demagoguery, creating its own 'alternative facts'; in this, the Kremlin far surpasses any right-wing populists across the world. Simply put, my classes were the place to honour the truth when truth is a rare commodity. This is why I have always considered teaching in Russia to be inherently political and treated it as such, vowing to stay for as long as I could.

Russian academia is a peculiar institution. Since the early 1990s, humanities and social sciences have been divided between the 'nativists' who prefer to do research (or, rather, what they call 'research') more or less in isolation from the outside world, and the 'globalists' who try to join the international academic discussion. For ➔

My classes were the place to honour the truth when truth is a rare commodity

Darkness has descended upon Russia. Military losses are compensated by the viciousness of internal repression

→ reasons of prestige, the government has promoted the 'globalist' sector. But the massive push to improve Russian universities' position in the international rankings coincided with the Kremlin's increasingly paranoid, hysterical nationalism of the 2010s. This created a schizophrenic situation in which the authorities saw the internationalisation of Russian science as both desirable and deeply suspect. Russian scholars were expected to publish in high-ranking journals and participate in joint projects with their foreign colleagues, and yet, foreign-grant financing was to a large extent criminalised and the international research cooperation was subject to multiple bureaucratic hurdles.

And then, of course, there was the question of politics. Those pesky scholars refused to do internationally acclaimed research while remaining safely Putinist in their views, as the government would have preferred them to. They engaged in political commentary, went to street rallies and demonstrated 'unruly' behaviour. Unable to bear any criticism, the government turned to purges, hence the attacks on the European University, Smolny College and others. Once again, a schizophrenic approach: in the year when the EUSP was closed down, it held the top spot in the official Ministry of Science ranking of research universities. The Higher School of Economics in Moscow, another successful post-Soviet institution, simply lost its political science department: the very discipline appeared to be dangerous to the regime. A new generation of Russian scholars could relive the Soviet experience in which they were fired for signing this or that open letter.

The students are another worry for the government. When I myself was a student in the 2000s, my classmates, with very few exceptions, were apolitical and overwhelmingly focused on private life – just like the rest of the Russian population. In my senior year at high school, I read Robert Merle's novel Behind The Glass about the student uprising in Paris in 1968. When I began my studies at Moscow State University, I craved something similar to the events described in the novel, but of course I was disappointed.

Things have changed in recent years, however. The new generation of Russian students is far more politically conscious and active. In fact, they could teach those Paris dreamers a thing or two. Doxa, which began as a student publication at the Higher School of Economics, is now a major voice against repression and war. At some point it was kicked out by the HSE's fearful administrators, but this did not stop its young editors and authors. During last year's wave of protests triggered by Alexei Navalny's investigation into Putin's palace and Navalny's imprisonment upon return to Russia, Doxa fought hard for students' rights, highlighting cases of expulsions from the universities across the country and providing legal advice. For that, four of its editors spent one year under house arrest and were eventually sentenced to two years of public works (see our interview with one of the Doxa Four on p.43). And yet, Doxa is still standing despite the constant threat of harsh prison sentences.

The war is a watershed moment for Russian academia. Gone are the days of the precarious balance and the attempts to have it both ways. International cooperation has come to a halt, the rankings game is essentially abandoned, wartime repression has made meaningful work more or less impossible and the economic shock will leave the already underfunded academic institutions without any resources. Some of the 'nativists' praise the victory of the 'indigenous' science that will supposedly thrive in isolation. The 'globalists' (namely proper scientists) are scared and demoralised. Many have left; many more will follow whenever they can. The dean of my department refused to sign a pro-war statement. He was threatened by the university administrators who demanded that he withdraw his signature from an anti-war letter. Instead, he resigned from his position. The department is now in shambles, just like many other social and political science departments across the country.

Darkness has descended upon Russia. Military losses are compensated by the viciousness of internal repression. I praise those of my colleagues who decided to stay – I know they will do everything in their power to continue teaching students the truth. For those who have left, two areas of work are of paramount importance. One is the attempt to establish free academic institutions outside Russia aimed at Russian students. I strongly believe these attempts should be supported by Europe: they are an investment in the future democratic Russia that will finally have a national reckoning with the crimes of war and empire. Another area is flexible online education aimed at those students who cannot leave Russia. Once again, every opportunity to speak the truth counts.

I do not know whether this forced emigration will allow me to shape Russia's future in any way. But I will try and I know I am not alone. ✖

Ilya Matveev is a Russian researcher and lecturer

51(02):40/42|DOI:10.1177/03064220221110758

Don't be afraid to say two plus two is four

ALLA GUTNIKOVA has been sentenced to corrective labour in Russia for her role in independent student publication Doxa. **MARK FRARY** spoke to her about her court statement, published below and why she was impelled to speak out

A S WE APPROACH the 50th anniversary of the publication of The Gulag Archipelago by Soviet dissident Aleksandr Solzhenitsyn, the idea of enforced labour for those who speak out against the government of Russian President Vladimir Putin seems to be raising its head again.

Border closures due to Covid and growing concerns over the number of foreigners in the country have seen the number of migrant workers from Central Asia, who have typically been used on large public infrastructure projects, plummet. Some feel the answer to this labour shortage lies in the growing number of prisoners in the country, with "correctional labour" used as an alternative to prison.

In June of 2021, for example, the country's prison service said convicts would be used to construct a new section of the Baikal-Amur Mainline track in Siberia. The announcement

raised concerns as the line had originally been built as part of the gulag system in the 1930s, which led to thousands of deaths.

The government insists it has no plans to return to the gulags of Stalin's time, but one thing these two eras have in common is the use of forced labour to punish and intimidate those who dissent. Among those carrying out such penalties are four student journalists who were sentenced in April to two years of correctional labour. Alla Gutnikova, Armen Aramyan, Volodya Metelkin and Natasha Tyshkevich of the independent student publication Doxa (from the Greek for "opinion") were sentenced for posting a YouTube video in which they said it was illegal to intimidate students for taking part in protests in support of Alexei Navalny, the jailed critic of Putin.

Gutnikova's reaction on hearing the sentence of two years' corrective labour was perhaps unexpected.

"I was so happy and thought about having a beer to celebrate. Corrective labour sounds scary – after all, we had the gulag in Russia. When people hear this they think they are going to take us away from our homes, put us in a camp and make us work like slaves," she told Index.

She believes the reality of correctional labour will not be as harsh. Anyone sentenced to corrective labour who has an official job must pay 20% of their salary to the government. If they do not have a job, the government will find them one, such as being a cleaner in

ABOVE: Armen Aramyan, Natasha Tyshkevich, Alla Gutnikova and Volodya Metelkin, journalists at the independent student publication Doxa, were convicted to two years of correctional labour in Russia

public buildings. "I was so scared they were going to put us in jail, and any corrective labour is better than prison," she said. "Nothing is worse than Russian prison."

Even though correctional labour might be a less brutal outcome than a Russian prison, the sentencing was rightly reported around the world as a dark day for media freedom in the country.

As part of their sentencing, the four journalists were permitted to make statements to the court but they chose not to plead for the judge's clemency.

Aramyan and Metelkin both spoke about the war in Ukraine, with the former holding a symbolic minute's silence for its victims and the latter talking of the death by Russian shelling of Kharkiv resident Boris Romanchenko, who had survived four concentration camps – including Buchenwald – in World War II.

Tyshkevich spoke about her year under house arrest, saying: "The state forcibly held me, confined me to the space of home, of family, and is trying to infantilise me. I appropriate these spaces for myself and remember all the practices of resistance to the system that I devised at school: to write ➔

> I was so scared they were going to put us in jail, and any corrective labour is better than prison

→ your own essays instead of their compositions, to elude surveillance, to dream of other worlds and, of course, to unite with others despite prohibitions and borders."

Gutnikova's statement was something else entirely. In her opening remarks she said she would not talk about "the case, the police raid, the interrogations, the court files, or the trials – this is boring and pointless". Instead, her statement (reproduced here) is a paean to the poets, authors, artists and activists, such as Bulat Okudzhava, Audre Lord, Joseph Brodksy and Ernest Hemingway, who have shaped her view that it is acceptable to say that the emperor has no clothes and that two plus two really does equal four.

Speaking to Index following her sentencing, Gutnikova said many Russians could not believe she had spoken out. She said: "The concept of *parrhesia*, outlined by French sociologist Michel Foucault in his lectures, means you decide to speak your mind when in front of someone who has power over you. For example, you come to a king and look him in the face and tell him the truth he doesn't want to hear. After you tell the truth you might be killed but the truth is more important than your personal safety."

It is a noble concept but fraught with risk in Putin's Russia.

"To be honest, when I was speaking I felt really weak, frightened and ashamed of my fear," she said, the emotion plain in her voice as she recalls the hearing.

Statement by Alla Gutnikova

I WON'T BE talking about the case, the police raid, the interrogations, the court files, or the trials – this is boring and pointless. Lately I've been attending the school of fatigue and frustration. Yet before my arrest, I managed to enrol in the school of knowing how to talk about truly important things.

I wish I could talk about philosophy and literature. About Benjamin, Derrida, Kafka, Arendt, Sontag, Barthes, Foucault, Agamben, Audre Lorde, and bell hooks. About Oxana Timofeeva, Madina Tlostanova and Maria Rakhmaninova. I wish I could talk about poetry. How to read contemporary poetry. I wish I could talk about Mikhail Gronas, Grigori Dashevsky and Vassia Borodin.

But this is neither the time nor the place. I will hide my small delicate words on the tip of my tongue, in the back of my throat, somewhere between my stomach and my heart. And I'll just say a few things.

I often feel like a little fish, a small bird, a school kid, or a baby. But recently I was astonished to learn that Brodsky, too, was only 23 at his trial. And since I, too, have been put in the ranks of humanity, I will say it like this:

In the Kabbalah there is the concept of *tikkun*

olam, the repair of the world. I see that the world is imperfect. I believe that, as Yehuda Amichai wrote, the world is beautifully made for doing good and for resting, like a park bench (a park bench, not a court bench!). I believe that the world was created for tenderness, hope, love, solidarity; for passion and joy.

But there is a terrible, unbearable amount of violence in the world. And I do not want violence. Not in any form. I do not want teachers' hands down schoolgirls' underwear. I do not want drunken fathers' fists beating the bodies of their wives and children. Were I to list all the violence that I am aware of, there would not be enough days, weeks or years. To start seeing violence one simply has to open their eyes. My eyes are open. I see the violence, and I do not want it. The more violence there is, the more I do not want it. And most of all I do not want the greatest, the most terrible violence.

I love to learn. From hereon I will speak in the voices of others.

In high school history lessons I learned sayings such as "You may crucify freedom, but the human soul knows no shackles" and "For your freedom and ours."

In high school I read Anna Akhmatova's Requiem, Yevgenia Ginzburg's Journey Into the Whirlwind, Bulat Okudzhava's The Closed-Down Theatre, Anatoly Rybakov's Children of the Arbat. I especially loved one poem by Okudzhava:

Gutnikova's statement has been widely shared since.

"When there is so much fear and no hope and everyone is on the edge of their mental capacity because of the catastrophe happening in front of our eyes, then maybe because the text was poetic and literary it gave people hope and strength," she said. "It was somehow a relief for them to read it."

The four journalists have also been banned from being involved in running websites for three years. But Doxa will continue, she said, despite the court-imposed ban.

"Maybe they thought if they caught four of us it would stop, but we didn't shut down and didn't stop work and there are lots of others who could work for Doxa. Now almost all of our editors are not in Russia and there is no censorship for them," she said.

Gutnikova believes it is vital for writers to continue to express themselves however they can.

"Even if you are silenced by your government, you still have to write – and maybe one day that could be published. You can use metaphors or try to be poetic to express your ideas but not give [the authorities] any evidence of your 'guilt'. In the USSR, many started writing kids' books."

Not writing is not an answer, she believes. "You don't have to stay silent – your silence will not protect you." ✖

Mark Frary is associate editor at Index on Censorship

Conscience, noble ways and dignity –
There it is, our sacred host.
Reach out your palms to it.
You'll walk fearless into fire for it.
Its visage lofty and amazing.
Devote to it your humble life:
You'll never be victorious,
But you'll die a human being!

At MGIMO University, I studied French and learned the line from Edith Piaf: "Ça ne pouvait pas durer toujours ["It could not last forever"]. And another from Marc Robin: "Ça ne peut pas durer comme ça" ["It can't go on like this"].

When I was 19, I went to Majdanek and Treblinka and learned how to say "never again" in seven ways: [Russian], never again, jamais plus, nie wieder, קיינמאל מער, nigdy więcej, לא עוד.

I studied the Jewish sages and there were two sayings that I came to love the most. Rabbi Hillel said: "If I am not for myself, who will be for me? If I am only for myself, what am I? And if not now, when?"

And then there was Rabbi Nachman, who said: "The whole world is a very narrow bridge and the main thing is to have no fear at all."

Then I entered the HSE School of Cultural Studies and learned a few more important lessons. First, words matter. Second, one has to call things by their proper names. And finally: sapere aude – have the courage to use your own mind.

It is ridiculous and absurd that our case has to do with schoolchildren. I have taught humanities to children in English, worked as a babysitter, dreamed of taking part in the Teach for Russia programme – of going away to a small town for two years and sowing the reasonable, the good, the eternal. But Russia, in the words of public prosecutor Tryakin, accuses me of involving minors in life-threatening activities. If I should ever have any children (which I definitely should have, because I do remember the greatest commandment), I'll hang on their wall a portrait of the Procurator of Judaea, Pontius Pilate, so that they will grow up neat and clean. Procurator Pontius Pilate standing there washing his hands – that's the right kind of portrait. Indeed, if thinking and not being indifferent is now life-threatening, I do not know what to say regarding the substance of the accusation. I wash my hands.

And now is the moment of truth. The now of legibility. My friends and I are all undone with horror and pain, but when I go down into the subway, I do not see faces streaked with tears. I do not see faces streaked with tears.

Of all my favourite books, not one – neither children's books, nor books for adults – taught me apathy, indifference, cowardice. Not one taught me phrases like these:

We are little people
I'm just a simple person
Nothing's that simple
You can't trust anyone   ➔

→ I'm not particularly interested in all that
I'm not involved in politics
None of this has anything to do with me
I can't change anything
The people in charge will deal with it
What could I have done about it on my own?
No, instead I know and love completely
different words.

Hemingway speaks in the words of John Donne:

No man is an Iland, intire of it selfe; every man is
a peece of the Continent, a part of the maine; if a
Clod bee washed away by the Sea, Europe is the
lesse, as well as if a Promontorie were, as well as
if a Mannor of thy friends or of thine owne were;
any mans death diminishes me, because I am
involved in Mankinde; And therefore never send
to know for whom the bell tolls; It tolls for thee.

Mahmoud Darwish says:

As you prepare your breakfast, think of others
(do not forget the pigeon's food).
As you conduct your wars, think of others
(do not forget those who seek peace).
As you pay your water bill, think of others
(those who are nursed by clouds).
As you return home, to your home, think of
others
(do not forget the people of the camps).
As you sleep and count the stars, think of others
(those who have nowhere to sleep).
As you liberate yourself in metaphor, think of
others
(those who have lost the right to speak).
As you think of others far away, think of yourself
(say: "If only I were a candle in the dark").

Gennady Golovaty says:

The blind cannot stare in rage.
The mute cannot scream in fury.
The armless cannot hold weapons.
The legless cannot march forward.
But: the mute can stare in rage.
But: the blind can scream in fury.

But: the legless can hold weapons.
But: the armless can march forward.

I know some people are afraid. They choose
silence.
    But Audre Lorde says: "Your silence will not
protect you."
    On the Moscow subway, the public
announcement says: "Passengers are forbidden to
stay on trains headed to a dead end."
    The lyrics by the Petersburg band Aquarium
continue: "This train is on fire."
    Tarkovsky speaks in the words of Lao Tzu:

"The most important thing is that they believe in
themselves and become as helpless as children.
Because weakness is great and strength is null.
At birth, people are supple and weak; at death,
they are tough and stiff. When trees grow they
are soft and flexible, and when they become dry
and hard, they die. Stiffness and strength are the
concomitants of death; softness and weakness
express the freshness of being. Thus what has
grown hard will not conquer."

Remember that fear eats the soul. Remember the
character from Kafka, who saw "a gallows being
set up in the prison yard, mistakenly thought it
was for him, escaped from his cell at night and
hanged himself". Be like little children. Do not be
afraid to ask (yourselves and others) what is good
and what is bad. Do not be afraid to say that
the emperor has no clothes. Do not be afraid to
scream, to burst into tears. Repeat (to yourselves
and to others): 2+2=4. Black is black. White is
white. I am a human, I am strong and brave. We
are strong and brave.
    Freedom is the process by which you develop a
practice for being unavailable for servitude. ✖

*Translated by **Karina Papp**, **Galina Ryazanskaya**,*
*and **Mikhail Konovalenko**, with Ivan Sokolov and*
Ainsley Morse

Alla Gutnikova *is one of the founders of Doxa*

51(02):43/46|DOI:10.1177/03064220221110759

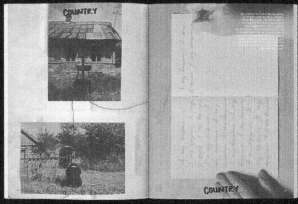

Emotional baggage

Celebrated Croatian journalist **SLAVENKA DRAKULIĆ** writes an exclusive essay on what a refugee should pack in their suitcase and how they must be prepared to learn a whole new language

YOU ARE LEAVING tomorrow; the time of deliberation has passed. Yesterday in the early morning hours, a house in the neighbourhood was bombed, and the smoke is still rising. An unknown, disturbing stench overwhelms you as soon as you open a window.

Now you are sitting in your darkened living room, with electricity long gone, looking at the suitcase gaping open on the floor. In Ukraine you call it *tryvozhna valizka*, an alarm suitcase, a suitcase of anxiety - a kind of suitcase of fear.

Slightly panicked, you throw in a warm pullover; you might need it, a neighbour told you, so you put it in and replace your favourite dress. Why would a refugee need a fancy dress? You ask yourself and throw it out. What to take with you? People tell you to take this and not forget that. Suddenly they all are experts on what it means to flee. But even if you could put in all you needed, from books and warm clothes to food →

Suddenly they all are experts on what it means to flee

→ and medicine, how would you carry such a heavy burden?

"Put on a solid pair of walking shoes," your grandma, your beloved *babusya*, would say. "You will surely walk a lot. My dear, *moya lyuba*," she would tell you. "Leave that bulky *valizka* here; there is nothing in it that can protect you from the war."

If only she were with you now. But her bones are at the cemetery, and it has not been hit yet. The Russian soldiers are targeting live Ukrainians for now, but soon the turn will come for the dead, too. Because the dead represent the memory of the living, they too have to be annihilated. "Don't ask what kind of people could kill the elderly, small children and their mothers - people kill people, we are doing it to each other. Now Russians kill us but believe me; we'll be killing them too." You know that her view of human nature was dark. But you also know that you can't command the dead to shut up; they tell you how to remember them. If you would angrily retort: this is not the time to compare, we are defending ourselves, *babusya* would simply wave her hand as if to say: I've seen it all; I know what the people are capable of.

"But they kill even cats!" You tell her, as perhaps the final argument against Russian soldiers. You found your Luna wounded in front of the door, and she died in your hands. Why? Animals are not enemies. You passed a dead shepherd dog on the way back from fetching the water; someone loved that dog as you loved Luna. You've stayed so long here because you could not imagine leaving her. It was while digging a shallow grave in the flower bed that you became certain that you wanted to leave all this behind. Strange, you think now, in the darkness lit by the single candle, how odd that what really scared you - the fact that soldiers had no mercy, even for animals - was what finally scared you away.

If only *Babusya* could help you now, as she used to do when you were a

child. In your mind, you can see her face leaning over to kiss your forehead; you can feel her warm hands, you can almost feel her presence. "Well, don't be sad, you can take your *valizka* with you. But not the one on the floor, not the one you used to take on vacation to Crimea. No, open another one, the one in your mind, the one for the images and memories, for the smell of spring and memory of a certain touch. That is the *valizka* you will need more as it can be filled by all you hold dear, everything you are. That invisible luggage will become your survival kit.

"And now, *moya lyuba*, before you leave, it is time to pick up the candle and have a good look around," she would say, directing you to the kitchen, with its neatly washed dishes and clean tablecloth. "Did you set it up for your return?" I did that out of habit, you would explain to her, and she would understand; she was the one who taught you to clean after yourself. In the living room, she would notice something that no one else would. The absence of photos, one of herself and your mother, the other of the entire family, usually proudly exposed on the dresser, under the clock. You took the pictures out of frames so that they will keep you company along the way. You apologetically say, in a weak voice; some of the pictures I have hidden in a safe place until I return. "Yes, I know every refugee believes that leaving home is only temporary; otherwise, how would they bear to leave?"

You hadn't intended to leave, even when shelling was getting closer, even when all the other neighbours from the apartment building had left, as if you believed the war would not touch you. How to desert the place where you and your parents worked hard to earn for

every single thing, from the big flat screen TV set to the fine new carpet? Lovely presents you got for your birthday, old inherited teacups, that fine coat you saved for, the small things that made you happy. Leaving home to save your life was unimaginable, for what is life without everything that makes it home?

You can almost feel *Babusya* reading your mind as you touch the cushions on the bed, the reading lamp and a new, unread book waiting for you to open. "Try to take the moments with you. Remember how you fell from a bicycle the first time you rode and hurt your knee but stubbornly climbed on again? Or buying a pair of red dancing shoes for your graduation?"

Other moments you won't be able to forget, even if you wish you could: the one when you spotted the first human corpse. It was only yesterday, you remember in amazement. As you walked into your street, someone was lying on the pavement in front of number five. As you approached, as you had to pass by, you saw the old school janitor, who never let you into the school even if you were only a minute late. Lying there in his pyjamas, he looked as if he was asleep. But who would choose to sleep on the pavement on a chilly spring morning? Even from where you stood, you could see that his eyes were open, and there was some smeared blood on his right temple. You suddenly felt trapped. You stopped and screamed into the space, not hoping for an answer: why? Why? But the answer came in a familiar voice: "Don't go around asking why; you are not a child anymore!"

Life is not things; it is the memory of those things, the only way to keep them with you. Now you understand why your mental *tryvozhna valizka* is more important than the one on the floor. The one that you would uselessly drag, pull or carry around, hugging it and never letting go, until you get so tired that you'd want to abandon it, throwing it into the first water that would be deep enough to swallow it.

The other *valizka*, on the other hand, is the one that will always remain, the one you take home or wherever you go when the war ends, and it will; every war does. That one is heavy in a different way. What else is inside, apart from the fear, images from the past and your memories of the precious moments? Everything that you learned since the war started: the sound of the air raid siren, the word "shelter", the damp smell of the cellars, the scent of fresh blood that reminds you of iron. Also, lessons that you have yet to learn. You'll discover that your home is not yours because the others have the power to take it from you. You'll realise that for the same reason your life is not your own. You'll learn to be afraid, and that fear is good. You'll learn to choose sides as well as to be pushed to the side you did not choose; you might even need to know how to hate. "Hatred" is something one easily learns in such a situation. It is the most terrible lesson in survival; you'll most certainly learn the word "survival" and its meaning. One can survive anywhere, something you'll learn while walking in a long line towards some border or a safe place. That word, besides many other previous unknowns, will be the main word in your *valizka*. A "safe place" is another important notion; it seems only yesterday you believed any place you felt good was safe. And the word luck will get a new definition; while you sit on the wet soil somewhere in the woods, covered by a tarp under fat drops of cold rainfall, you'll suddenly

realise your luck. You'll experience the birth of a whole new dictionary born out of the war. You should carefully take those newly born words and keep them in your *valizka*, which is becoming more and more precious the further you go.

"I am telling you, it was a good idea to toss a photo of your house into your backpack. And you ask me why, again? Haven't you yet learned that war doesn't allow asking stupid questions? It's because you are homeless now, a refugee. I see, *lyuba*, that you disagree, fiddling with the house key in your pocket as if it proves something. You probably don't, but I remember an old newspaper photo - many years after the war in Bosnia ended. Every Saturday in Berlin, near Wittemberg, one could see the same scene: women, many women, standing silently, each holding a photo, closeups of their houses, of homes they once had until the others appropriated them. Or shelled them, burned them. The women held the photos as the only proof, as the document that they, too, lived a different life just like the rest of us. That's what I am saying. I remember how it hit me, the idea that an image of the house could be the proof of belonging to ordinary people. Such a photo, not a house key, became an essential identity document, just like an ID card.

"You are that kind of a refugee now, do you understand?"

It is a new word as well, but after a week, you will realise that this single word sums up what you are to others. It will take time to see yourself as a refugee because the picture it evokes is usually quite different. A big mass of people, women with headscarves, young men, children, walking or waiting, sitting on the ground

or crouching under the open sky somewhere at the Hungarian border, expecting a transport to Germany, their skin darker than yours. Surely you remember the picture of a dead Syrian refugee boy lying on a beach in Turkey; it sent a shudder down your spine. Soon you will learn that your Ukrainian nationality and the pale skin colour will decide your destiny, as his nationality and skin colour did his.

Once you are safe and taken care of in a new country, you will experience a strange feeling; a confusing mixture of gratitude to your benefactors and a kind of a shame at the same time. That is because it is not easy to receive charity. You are in need, and to be needy is humiliating. Charity is perhaps the heaviest of burdens.

"Trust me; you are not alone. My bones will stay here, but I will live on in your *valizka*. But here is one last thing I must warn you about before letting you go. You might see a few dead people along the way and start to think you know death because you can feel the cold sweat of fear. That is not what I mean. You need to do better, recognise the mortal danger, its icy breath just behind you, without seeing its face. This skill, not things you took from home, will save your life. Learn it fast, *moya lyuba...*" *Babusya*'s voice is fading.

Now you can see the pale light of dawn breaking. The sign for you to leave.

Leave the heavy suitcase of fear, leave it there, open on the floor.

Don't cry.

Smile as you close the door, you are no longer burdened by fears, but strengthened by what you carry inside, and nobody can take from you.

You are as set as any refugee could ever be. ✖

Slavenka Drakulić is a journalist and writer whose books have been translated into many languages. She was born in Croatia (then Yugoslavia) in 1949

Hatred is something one easily learns in such a situation

51(02):48/51|DOI:10.1177/03064220221110760

BATTLE FOR UKRAINE

Back to the future

Cutting through the noise and providing vital information from the Ukrainian frontline is crucial. **MARTIN BRIGHT** talks to two broadcasters about learning lessons from the past

"UNLIKE IN THE seventies and eighties, you have an abundance of entertainment and abundance of noise and abundance of misinformation and disinformation that is much, much more appealing than whatever propaganda there was out there in that broadcast era." Patrick Boehler, head of digital strategy at Radio Free Europe/Radio Liberty, is discussing the future of journalism with Index in the context of the war in Ukraine. Although he understands why people are quick to draw parallels with the Cold War, he is keen to insist on some fundamental differences. He continued:

"One of the things we really think about when we publish is what are the information needs of the audience that we serve, so that they can make political decisions and navigate their daily lives. Because essentially, that element of scarcity that existed in the Cold War is no longer there."

One indicator for Boehler, an Austrian journalist and former diplomat, is downloads of virtual private networks. These apps permit computer users to hide their identity online, enabling them to browse the internet securely

LEFT: Journalists and military personnel in Mariupol in Ukraine, April 2022

local level. Lessons learned during the pandemic have proved useful during the Ukraine war. RFE/RFL found that people in Russia were desperate to find accurate information about the spread of Covid-19 and the availability of vaccinations and hospital treatment. They have applied the same principle to getting information into Russia, whether it concerns the level of inflation or where troops from a particular part of the country are being sent in Ukraine.

Radio Free Europe was established in 1950 to broadcast behind the Iron Curtain in Bulgaria, Czechoslovakia, Hungary, Poland, and Romania. Three years later, Radio Liberty started broadcasting to the Soviet Union. Although initially funded by the CIA, this set-up ended in 1971. RFL/RL now functions as a single non-profit organisation funded by a grant from Congress. It operates in 27 languages in 23 countries with over 600 staff journalists and 1,300 freelancers. The organisation has benefitted from a thirst for information free from hyperbole and misinformation. Its YouTube channel now boasts around 400 million views, up 153% on the same period last year. Its websites have nearly 32 million unique users, a rise of 41% (despite Russian blocking).

In Ukraine, the media organisation has quickly had to adapt to the new landscape: using TikTok to track the movements of troops across Russia as they make their way to the front line in the Donbass region, tracing →

and anonymously. In authoritarian regimes such as Russia or Belarus, VPNs have allowed journalists, activists and ordinary citizens to access material censored by their own government. It has also meant these "digital dissidents" are able to distribute "digital *samizdat*" in ways their predecessors in the Cold War era could only dream about.

"Even in Turkmenistan, if you look at the app store downloads, you will see that the most downloaded apps are always VPNs," said Boehler. "And once you have the VPN, you have an abundance of content out there."

The question for Boehler is how you then persuade this audience to focus on the content provided by RFE/RL rather than anything else. The answer, he feels, is to concentrate on information that will be useful on a

These "digital dissidents" are able to distribute "digital samizdat" in ways their predecessors in the Cold War era could only dream about

The process of shifting onto a war footing has not been without its ethical problems for Hromadske, particularly when it comes to the security of its journalists

→ the London-based assets of Putin's oligarch backers and identifying the personnel of the doomed warship, the Moskva. But at the same time, RFE/RL has had to fight the idea that it is simply an arm of the US government and its journalists therefore foreign agents.

Simple denial is not an option for Boehler: "In a way we then risk unintentionally amplifying and validating these narratives," he said. "So instead of doing that, we asked our Siberian journalists, for example, tell us, why did you become a journalist? What motivates you? Why do you do all this despite the risks of prosecution, which now amounts to being given treason charges? And, you know why? Because they want Siberia to be a better place."

Understandably, Boehler is not prepared to discuss the security arrangements for the journalists working for RFE/RL. But he pays tribute to the local staff who face risks on an everyday basis: "We have 23 news rooms. They are in Afghanistan and Pakistan, up to Hungary. These teams have their own very able reporters and editors and they have very diverse reporting focuses in terms of topics that are relevant in the various countries. We have fantastic teams serving Russia. And I think it's really one of those moments where you see our journalists living up to the task and the challenge that they face. And it's really inspiring."

In many ways, the imperatives for Yevheniia Motorevska, editor-in-chief at the independent Ukrainian broadcaster Hromadske (Public) are the same as for RFE/RL: providing up-to-date information in a complex conflict zone while keeping its staff of reporters and producers on the ground safe from harm. But its approach could not be

more different. Working with just five reporters, the tiny operation does not have the capacity to work with the latest developments in open-source intelligence or data journalism. Instead, it has thrown everything into old-fashioned war reporting.

"Before the war, we covered political and social topics, but now the working conditions have changed dramatically," said Motorevska. "We don't cover any topics other than the war now. We have no political or social journalists; they are all war reporters."

Using a stripped-down operation working via its own website and YouTube channel, Hromadske produces pieces from the combat zone that attract more than two million views for an audience desperate for up-to-the-minute news from the frontline. Recent reports have concentrated on fighting in the east of the country with a recent report on a successful operation to repulse a tank attack near Donetsk one of the most viewed in the history of Hromadske.

When war broke out, the broadcaster was forced to abandon its English-language website, but in recent weeks, the service has been back online with reports on life under Russian occupation in the southern Ukrainian city of Enerhodar, interviews with foreign fighters and the war diary of a young woman deported from Mariupol after her parents were killed in the shelling of the city.

The process of shifting onto a war footing has not been without its ethical problems for Hromadske, particularly when it comes to the security of its journalists. In the early weeks of the war Index published accounts of Hromadske reporter Viktoria Roshchina, who was kidnapped by

Russian troops while travelling to report on the occupation of Mariupol. When Roshchina decided not to take up an offer of trauma counselling after release, Motorevska decided it was too dangerous to let her continue working with Hromadske. Roshchina has since reported for RFE/RL on the Russian May 9th victory parade in Mariupol and for the online news service Ukrainska Pravda.

As in other areas of life, the war in Ukraine has led to a spirit of cooperation that has, at times, even curtailed the endless search for exclusivity. Boehler, himself a seasoned reporter in Hong Kong and China, has noted this change and believes it is a positive development: "[The conflict] really has shown the need for collaboration and solidarity amongst journalists," he said. "We as journalists were trained to have a scoop, to beat everyone to a story. That is, of course, very satisfying, but what really matters is serving an audience and being useful by giving them the information they need."

It will take some time to adjust to the new journalistic landscape. What will the consequences be for Ukrainian civil society, for example, now its investigative journalists have turned their attention from corruption to war crime? And even in wartime, can journalists really be expected to suppress their natural professional competitiveness in order to provide "useful" information. Journalists are entertainers as well as mere news providers, as RFE/RL and Hromadske will need to recognise if they want to cut through in this age of information abundance. ✖

Martin Bright is editor-at-large at Index

51(02):52/54|DOI:10.1177/03064220221110761

On not being shot

JOHN SWEENEY spent the first few months of the war in Kyiv. Here he pays tribute to some of the remarkable people, including journalists, he met

FIVE RUSSIAN CRUISE missiles hit Kyiv while the UN secretary-general was still in town. Three were knocked out of the sky by the Ukrainian air defence system, one hit some houses close to a railway line but the fifth punched into the base of a block of flats in the centre of the capital at 500 miles per hour, killing Radio Free Europe/Radio Liberty reporter Vira Hyrych.

The Kremlin's respect for free speech, for the rule of law and the international community could not have been more succinctly expressed. Hyrych's last story was to work on a video interview of Elvira Borts, a Holocaust survivor, 87 years old, who lived through both the Nazi and Russian sieges of Mariupol and found the one in 2022 more dreadful. And then the journalist who tells her story is blown to smithereens.

After months in Kyiv, I will soon return home to London to reflect on what I learnt from my Ukrainian friends. I feel a mixture of great anger at so many in the West who took Moscow's dirty gold for too long and great pride in getting to know amidst Kyiv's cramped hospital basements and crowded tube stations during the worst of days the aristocracy of the human soul.

I will remember going to Kyiv Children's Hospital to follow up a story about children with cancer hiding in the basement. They had pretty much all gone but we stumbled into another group of sick kids, those on kidney dialysis machines. If they leave the

machines to get out, they may die. If they stay in Kyiv, they may die. And in the middle of this was Chou-Chou the clown, herself a refugee from Donetsk, cracking jokes, confusing the name of Alyona, a slightly prim thirteen-year-old girl, with "Elon Musk", and the very idea of Mr Tesla being in that dark place at that dark time made Alyona and I weep with laughter.

I will remember the people from the morgue picking up the remains of a mother and a child killed in the rocket attack on the TV Tower, getting a blanket to give the dead some dignity, doing their grim job properly.

I will remember two young men in Bucha putting the dead in body-bags. One civilian had been shot in the back of the head; a second shot in the face. We have not identified the first man but Ukrainian journalist Liza Kozlenko managed to find out the name of the second, Alexander Fedorov. He was a builder, working on a job in Bucha when the war came. He was an only child. His mother is bereft.

When people suggest that Ukraine talks peace with the Kremlin, how can you compromise with those whose manners are shooting an unarmed man in the face? Eh?

I suspect that some of my judgments about the Kremlin's killing machine would not have been approved by my old bosses at the BBC. But now journalism has changed. I could not have stayed in Kyiv so long without fellow Britons and others around the world supporting my journalism through the membership service Patreon and by crowdfunding my podcast, Taking On Putin. I came with no kit, no Patrons and no backers. Now independent journalists have another way of telling truth to power and it's sweet and smart.

Reflecting on the Chinese Communist Party, a very long time ago, His Holiness The Dalai Lama told me: "the enemy is the best teacher." The Kremlin's message is clear: do what you're told. Or else. I have seen too much Ukrainian (and Russian) blood spilt to ever forget that.

Once again, with feeling: free speech does not come free. ✖

John Sweeney is an author and reporter

51(02):55/55|DOI:10.1177/03064220221110762

RIGHT: Rescuers carry the body of Radio Free Europe/Radio Liberty reporter Vira Hyrych, who was killed in an airstrike in Kyiv, Ukraine 29 April, 2022

BATTLE FOR UKRAINE

Russia's Trojan horse moves closer to Europe

Hungary's right-wing president secured another term in power through manipulating the Ukraine war narrative. **VIKTÓRIA SERDÜLT** fears for the country's future

A FEW HOURS AFTER polling stations closed in Hungary's general elections, Prime Minister Viktor Orbán greeted supporters outside his Fidesz party's election headquarters, on the banks of the Danube. Dressed in his signature orange tie and surrounded by his closest political allies, he addressed the crowd after winning his fourth consecutive victory.

To chants of "Viktor, Viktor", Orbán thanked his followers for leading him to victory, but also sent a message to his "opponents", of which the president of Ukraine was listed as one.

As the EU's closest ally to Russian president Vladimir Putin, it was no surprise that Orbán name-checked

Volodymyr Zelensky. In the run-up to the election, Orbán tried to cast a February visit to Moscow as a "peace mission" and claim a vote for him was a vote for stability while a vote for the opposition was a vote for war.

With Hungary sharing a border with Ukraine, and its chances of becoming embroiled in the war therefore being much more than just an abstract possibility, his careful positioning – bolstered by a media that spun Kremlin propaganda – was a success.

And now Hungarians must brace themselves for further restrictions to their free expression.

Orbán's victory was big – bigger than ever before – so he can now basically rule the country as he wishes. During his previous terms, Fidesz used its powers to consolidate control over the country's judiciary, take over the media and universities, pass anti-immigrant and anti-LGBTQI laws, and crack down on non-governmental organisations critical of the government. That approach – leading Freedom House to list Hungary as only "partly free" in its global Freedom in the World Index – is unlikely to change.

Orbán drew strong criticism from the EU for trampling on human rights, but such concerns have not resonated with Hungarian voters. That is partly because the majority of them do not consider democracy and the rule of law to be their main priority. In a major 2021 poll by Policy Solutions and the Friedrich Ebert Foundation, the most significant

Orbán's messaging does not send a positive signal to Hungary's vulnerable groups

CREDIT: Eva Voneki/Alamy

ABOVE: A poster of Hungary's Prime Minister Viktor Orbán before the parliamentary elections in April 2022, which reads: "Let's preserve the peace and security of Hungary!"

issues facing the country included poverty, the state of health care, low pensions and the cost of living.

The prime minister may have never previously won with such a large majority, but neither has he faced such a tough period in power. Inflation, rapidly rising living costs and soaring energy prices will soon take a serious toll on the Hungarian economy.

The government has already taken steps to minimise the effects of this, including extending a price cap on basic food products and fuel. But if Orbán really wants to stay in power, he needs to do what he is best at: hide the harsh reality from his voters and divert their →

Telex tells it all

Hungary's crowdfunded journalists stand tall against state control, writes **CHRIS MATTHEWS**

VERONIKA MUNK IS on a train bound for Budapest. She is returning from Prague where a sobering assessment on press freedom in the region was delivered the previous day.

In the most detailed study yet of the Visegrád countries (the Czech Republic, Hungary, Poland and Slovakia), researchers found widespread concern for media independence, with 43% of those surveyed in Hungary believing their media is not free.

For Munk, who spoke at the event about the situation in Hungary, which now ranks 85th in the Reporters Without Borders Press Freedom Index, the cause is an intensely personal one. In June 2020, she and her colleagues at news site Index.hu found their own operation under threat.

"Now there is trouble," read an online post by Index.hu journalists. "The staff and independence of Index are in grave danger."

A prominent critic of the state, Index.hu had grown to become Hungary's largest independent news platform. But after a pro-government businessman took a 50% stake in the firm controlling Index's advertising, staff feared for their futures. Those fears crystalised soon after when editor-in-chief Szabolcs Dull was abruptly fired. Index.hu's 80-strong staff felt they were left with no alternative.

"The whole newsroom quit," said Munk, who spent 18 years at Index.hu, going from intern to deputy editor-in-chief. "It was a horrible moment because everybody had difficulties in their life, but we thought it was not OK anymore, and not possible for us to operate at an independent, professional level.

"The same day we quit there was a large protest in Budapest. Thousands of people were marching for us, and we realised: 'OK, these people need us'."

Three months later and with 70 former Index.hu staff onboard, Telex.hu launched. Early editorial meetings were held in coffee shops and parks and their first office was a disused school.

"We didn't care, though," said Munk, Telex's head of content development and founding editor-in-chief. "Because we could do what we wanted to do and provide fact-based news for Hungarians."

To deliver its "correct, critical and curious journalism", Telex – where Dull is now editor-in-chief – relies almost entirely on crowdfunding. It raised €1m in the first month, and it has more than 50,000 donors at home and abroad and around 600,000 daily readers.

"We now have one of the largest newsrooms in the country and we are flexible, we travel everywhere," Munk said. "We have had eight Telex staff in Ukraine since the war started and we believe in spending the money on good journalism."

Prime Minister Viktor Orbán's far-right Fidesz party, re-elected in April, has steadily eroded press freedoms and space for good journalism since he first won power in 2010. Laws have been passed limiting access to public information, leading independent newspaper Népszabadság to close in 2016, and it emerged last year that Hungarian journalists were among those targeted by the Pegasus spyware tool.

Media plurality has crumbled further since the Central European Press and Media Foundation (Kesma), an organisation staffed by pro-Fidesz figures, launched in 2018. Kesma controls nearly 500 media outlets, and it is estimated that nearly 90% of state advertising spend goes to Kesma and other Orbán-aligned channels.

"Kesma has this centralised way of spreading the political messaging of the government," said Munk. "It affects how people think about events in the country and outside."

Telex, though, and other independent voices such as radio station Klubrádió – another victim of the state's quest to monopolise the media landscape but which now runs an online station with its own crowdfunded model – continue to question narratives and populist propaganda.

"It seems our story has really convinced people to support the cause of press freedom," said Munk.

Chris Matthews is a freelance journalist based in London

Although he has voted for every EU sanction imposed on Russia, Orbán has been careful not to antagonise Putin

→ attention to less pressing subjects.

What these subjects may be are not hard to guess. Orbán – who has built his whole communications strategy on the "protection of Hungarians" – listed the domestic and international left, Brussels, George Soros and the international "mainstream media" as his opponents, alongside Zelensky.

Emboldened by his sweeping victory, there is a serious risk that Orbán will further challenge his opponents, including the EU, as the European Commission has for the first time in its history launched a conditionality mechanism against Hungary, meaning the country could be stripped of EU money for breaching democratic values.

The commission is worried about "systemic irregularities, deficiencies and weaknesses in public procurement procedures", but the Hungarian government is once again using the fight to blame Brussels for interfering with "the will of the Hungarian people".

Orbán's messaging does not send a positive signal to Hungary's vulnerable groups, including the LGBTQI community.

His government has already argued that the commission wants to punish it for staying out of the Ukraine war and for defending children from "sexual propaganda" – hinting at a series of anti-LGBTQI measures that were put into law last year. Civil rights activists fear that a new battle with Brussels over money could make LGBTQI people scapegoats at home.

Journalists worry that Fidesz will exert even more control over the media if the party wants to divert attention from the economic and social troubles. Convincing voters that government policies – including austerity measures

– are justified could lead to even stronger propaganda, says Ágnes Urbán, an analyst at Mérték Media Monitor.

"In the shorter term, a calmer period may be expected, simply because there will be no need for propaganda until the European Parliament elections in 2024. But there is a possibility it may intensify over time," she told Index.

"In previous years, the economy grew with the help of EU funds, [and] living standards increased in many layers of society. The main question is what to expect in a new economic situation, especially in the absence of EU subsidies. It is possible that the ruling party will try to hide the real processes from the population with increasingly intense propaganda in the long term."

There are already signs of this happening. At the end of May, the government amended the Fundamental Law for the tenth time, making it possible to declare a "state of danger" because of the armed conflict and humanitarian catastrophe in Ukraine. Orbán then quickly declared a state of danger, which means that his government can enact laws by decree without parliamentary oversight for a period of 15 days.

Originally created during the Covid-19 pandemic, the law allows the punishment of "spreading fake news" with up to five years in prison. In 2020, police detained an opposition activist and a pensioner for publishing their opinions on Facebook on the basis of the very same law. And though no charges were brought against them, their cases were proof of how the government can intimidate civilians.

Even more worrying is that Orbán's huge victory will encourage him to maintain his close ties with Putin. The Russian president may be a pariah in

most of Europe and the USA but not so much for Orbán, who depends on Moscow for cheap energy – something that was crucial in winning his election. And although he has voted for every EU sanction imposed on Russia, Orbán has been careful not to antagonise Putin. He refused to transfer lethal weapons to Ukraine through Hungary and has come out against oil and gas embargoes.

It's possible there may soon be no allies of Orbán other than eastern European autocrats. In March, two members of the Visegrád Four group of central European nations pulled out of their planned summit in Budapest. Soon afterwards, Hungary's closest EU ally, Poland, criticised Orbán's stance on Ukraine. (The Hungarian prime minister was also the only leader of the group not to travel to Kyiv to support Zelensky.)

With the fall of Janez Janša in Slovenia, Emmanuel Macron's re-election in France ending the presidential ambitions of nationalist Marine Le Pen, and the German government welcoming the European Commission's action against Hungary, it seems that Orbán has no allies left within the EU.

There are now fears that the increasing international isolation will push Orbán to forge even closer ties with Moscow. With Hungary long considered by many to be Russia's Trojan horse within the EU, there is no doubt that an increase in Moscow's influence will lead Hungary into an impossible position as far as its membership of the EU is concerned. With no friends left in Brussels, Orbán might feel he has only one option.

As one politician put it behind closed doors: "There is a real fear that Hungary will readily embrace a new normal, and that new normal in this case would be a return to Vladimir Putin and the prospect of cheap Russian oil." ✖

Viktória Serdült is a journalist based in Budapest

51(02):56/58|DOI:10.1177/03064220221110763

BATTLE FOR UKRAINE

Turkey's newfound Russophilia

The 'Eurasianist' movement in Turkey is manipulating the Ukraine war narrative to suit Putin, which is bad news for the country's fledgling freedoms, writes **KAYA GENÇ**

ON THE FOURTH week of Russia's invasion of Ukraine, one of Turkey's leading pollsters, Metropoll, published a striking statistic. In answer to the question "Who do you hold responsible for the events in Ukraine?", 48.3% of Turkish citizens pointed the finger at Washington and NATO. There were even people who said Ukraine was responsible for its woes: 7.5%. Just a third of those polled found Russia culpable for the havoc the country's army has been wreaking inside its sovereign neighbour since 24 February.

Turkey's newfound Russophilia is undiagnosed and widespread. Over the past half-decade, the government has prosecuted its critics using methods imported from the Kremlin. Vigilante groups assault opposition MPs on public avenues with kicks and punches and walk free afterwards. Ankara controls more than 90% of the Turkish media; its arsenal of newspapers and broadcasters uniformly disseminates government talking points around the clock. There are plans to classify Turkish freelancers working for Western media organisations as "foreign agents". This year, Turkey's constitutional court will judge whether to close HDP, an opposition party.

The assault on Turkey's progressive NGOs has a strong whiff of Putinism, too: The Open Society Foundation in Turkey ceased its operations in November 2018. Osman Kavala, in jail over the past half-decade, has widely been portrayed as "the Turkish collaborator of Soros". Prosecutors charged Kavala with organising the Gezi Park protests of 2013, which, like

Ukraine's Orange Revolution from 2004, has been portrayed by conspiracists as a "foreign-funded operation". For this he has been sentenced to life in prison without parole.

Turkish autocracy has never resembled its Russian counterpart more strongly.

Suat Kınıklıoğlu, a former MP from Turkey's ruling AKP, thinks Eurasianist organisations are behind this shift. But who are they? Founded by White Russian opponents of the Bolshevik Revolution in the 1920s, Eurasianism is a fiercely anti-European political movement. Its defenders argue that Russia isn't European. Instead, it belongs to a different continent: Eurasia, a standalone civilisation that can take over Europe, merge with Asia and form the world's largest continent under a Russian umbrella. Characterised by a deep-seated resentment of European values, Eurasianism entered Turkey in the 1990s, after the collapse of Soviet Russia, via the Workers Party, a fringe ultra-nationalist movement. Over the 2000s, Eurasianism became influential among high-ranking officials in the Turkish General Staff who opposed Ankara's entry to the EU, defending stronger ties with Russia and China instead.

Eurasianists boast anti-imperialism but remain silent on Russia's foreign interventions. In a report penned for the German Institute for International and Security Affairs, Kınıklıoğlu argued that Eurasianism's "real contribution

to the current regime comes from its critical role in widening and solidifying consent to authoritarian rule in Turkey. Containing a "blinding hatred of the West", the discourse has solidified into the "cement that holds together members of Turkey's governing coalition."

The far-right Russian strategist Alexander Dugin is one of the ideological architects of Turkey's inclusion in the Eurasian utopia. In his 1997 work, The Foundations of Geopolitics, Dugin presented Turkey as an adversary and a "political-ideological colony" of the USA that Russia needed to counter. Kınıklıoğlu notes how his views changed "as Turkey's relationship with Russia deepened, and Dugin's prestige increased in Turkish political circles who increasingly shared his deep-seated anti-Westernism." In 2003, Dugin's visit to Turkey for a Eurasia symposium garnered much media attention; by the time Dugin came to the capital Ankara in 2016 to visit the grave of Abdülhakim Arvasi, an Islamist sheikh whose worldview has shaped the thinking of the AKP's leadership, the Eurasian influence of Dugin on Turkey had peaked.

Since 1951, Turkey has been a NATO member, so it's unnerving to see NATO-trained Turkish generals wax poetic about Russia's revolutionary invasion on Turkish networks. "Turkey's talk show generals sway public against NATO" was the headline of a recent →

 Despite the Putinisation of Turkish politics, there is a silver lining

→ Middle East Eye investigation. As pro-government broadcasters breathlessly push the Kremlin line, public opinion has taken its inevitable, anti-Western shape. Meanwhile, similar sentiments reigned in the upper echelons of power, a pro-government businessman, Ethem Sancak, saying in March: "The main culprit in the Ukraine issue is NATO. It is a cancer. We won't join the sanctions against Russia because if Russia falls, Turkey could be partitioned." In May, Ankara said it would oppose Finland

and Sweden's bids to join NATO. Turkey's Eurasianists have defended Slobodan Milošević during the Bosnian War in 1995 and campaigned for Marine Le Pen in this year's elections.

The economy explains Eurasianism's ascent. As of writing, Ankara is Moscow's second-largest gas market after Berlin. Among the most significant Russian investments is the Akkuyu nuclear plant, whose agreement was signed in 2010 with an estimated cost of $20 billion. Planned to produce 10%

of Turkey's electricity needs, the plant is operated by Rosatom, which will own Akkuyu for 25 years. Turkey's import dependency on natural gas stood at 99% in 2017, and Ankara purchases 52% of its natural gas from Moscow, according to Soli Özel and Gökçe Uçar's study The Economics of Turkey-Russia Relations.

Yet, dig deeper, and you'll find, behind layers of economic ties, signs of animosity. In 2015, a Turkish F-16 downed a Russian SU-24 fighter jet that it claimed had violated Turkey's

ABOVE: Erdogan and Putin at the opening ceremony of Turkey's first nuclear power plant, Akkuyu Nuclear Power Plant, on 3 April 2018 in Turkey's southern Mersin province

air space: a camera captured the moment a Turkish militant shot the co-pilot while he was parachuting to safety. Russian sanctions ensued; Kremlin disinformation accused Turkey of funding ISIS; and Russia-Turkey relations were put on ice. Worryingly for Moscow, Turkey also supported the rebels in the Syrian civil war. As Turkey's President Recep Tayyip Erdoğan worked diligently to dethrone Bashar al-Assad, Islamists fumed at Putin for his intervention in September 2015 that saved the regime in Damascus.

"Turks can have two completely contradictory thoughts in their minds and be okay with voicing both," Soli Özel, a professor of international relations at Istanbul's Kadir Has University, told Index. "If Turks hate Assad so much, which they do, then they shouldn't support Russia. If they can say nothing to a country that killed 34 Turkish soldiers in Syria in 2020 in an airstrike, then, of course, Kremlin will treat Turkey like this."

But Eurasianism is an ideology autocrats adore. According to Karabekir Akkoyunlu from SOAS, University of London, the Turkish government relies on Russia to remain in power, an extraordinary relationship he dubs "a Faustian bargain" which has recently led to the promotion of Eurasianists to the highest places in government and the bureaucracy.

Since then, the former foes of Erdoğan have directed their pro-Slavic, anti-Islam anger away from the Turkish president; in return, the AKP keeps silent about human rights violations in Syria and China, and has invented a new mantra, *yerli ve milli* ("local and national"), that considers freedom of expression, parliamentary democracy and human rights as nefarious tools of the imperialist West.

Despite the worrying authoritarian trend, Turkey remains different from Russia, says Akkoyunlu. "We have a long memory and experience of democracy. Democratic institutions

Turkish autocracy has never resembled its Russian counterpart more strongly

aren't built in one day and can't be dismantled in a day either. Russia, meanwhile, has had no experience of democracy in the 20th century, but we know what it is." A significant difference is that Moscow's power comes mainly from the country's natural resources. "Russia is a rentier state. Luckily, Turkey doesn't have similar resources," Akkoyunlu said. "While Putin can use natural resources to consolidate his autocracy, we're fortunately poor in that field." As a result, while Turkey's current economic difficulties offer a glimmer of hope for the opposition to take power in next year's presidential elections, the same can't be said for resource-rich Russia.

But similarities between the regimes are increasing at a worrying rate, too. In 2018, complying with the Eurasian handbook, Turkey parted with its two-centuries long history of parliamentary democracy. The new presidential system, Akkoyunlu said, has brought the worst of both worlds: it destroyed stability, minimised prosperity and crushed democratic freedoms. Instead, the government rhetoric is based wholly on resentment. LGBTQI communities and the so-called "elites" who want the republic to remain true to its Westernising foundations are targeted daily, alongside scholars who oppose the government's permanent posturing and bullying.

Despite the Putinisation of Turkish politics, there is a silver lining. The war in Ukraine can serve as a mirror to Turkey, a reminder of autocracy's perils that also shows the extent of Russian influence in Turkey. "The invasion reveals the outcome of regimes where nobody can tell the leader that they're making a mistake," said Soli Özel, who hopes Russia's actions will show Turks that "a leader who is unaccountable is

not something to be proud of."

Opposition politicians are taking notice. Kemal Kılıçdaroğlu, the leader of the CHP party, has proclaimed: "NATO is not only a security institution but also a guardian of democracy." His ally Meral Akşener of the Good Party has asked Ankara to "wriggle itself out of the asymmetric relationship it has built with Russia." The AKP's former economy tsar Ali Babacan, who now leads DEVA Party, demanded his former boss act as "a dignified member of various European institutions would and should do."

Civil society is taking action, too. Turkey's Union of Chambers of Turkish Architects and Engineers had gone to court to stop the construction of the Akkuyu nuclear plant, operated by the Russian state corporation Rosatom. Turkey's Industry and Business Association (TUSIAD) has called to use the Ukrainian crisis to "undo the prevailing perceptions that Turkey moves away from the West and democratic principles, and that it is no longer a reliable member within NATO or the Council of Europe."

Akkoyunlu sees the Eurasianist resentment for the West as "part of our ontological insecurity" that is "intermixed with a desire to get the West's praises and a hunger for recognition by the West. They're the two faces of the same coin." Secret, passionate love for the West lies behind Turkey's Eurasianist posturing, in other words. In time, that anger may turn into love, illiberalism into democracy, oppression and censorship into liberty and freedom of expression. ✖

Kaya Genç is a contributing editor at Index. He is based in Istanbul

51(02):59/61|DOI:10.1177/03064220221110769

Divided by age and a TV screen

HANNA KOMAR writes on the challenges of speaking honestly about the war in Ukraine with her parents in Belarus

"WHEN RUSSIA INVADED Ukraine, I received a call from my mum, 'The TV is showing us something… How to react to this, tell me?' 'Russia invaded Ukraine,' I said. 'Got you,' she replied. 'This is madness.' My mother knows her daughter can be emotional but would never speculate with facts or manipulate someone's opinion. It's a choice, and she chooses to trust me." These were the words of a friend of mine, a London-based journalist with Belarusian roots, whose parents live in Estonia. When she told me this, I felt grateful to her mother for listening and being open to the truth. For most Belarusians, who have experienced decades of living under a dictator, talking about the war in Ukraine has been a source of familial conflict, torn as they are between truth and an avalanche of lies.

On 2 March 2022, a week into the Russian war in Ukraine, I talked to my own mum, telling her I was going to demonstrations in support of Ukraine in London every day. "Why do you support Ukraine and not Russia?" Her question felt like a bomb exploding.

One of the things I've heard from my mother over the years has been, "I don't understand anything about politics." I've

Friends for all the wrong reasons

The president of Belarus, Alyaksandr Lukashenka, is Vladimir Putin's closest ally. Recent events show they might only be getting closer, writes Guilherme Osinski

1 The fraudulent 2020 presidential elections in Belarus were met with international outcry as observers called foul play. With a ruthless response to protesters and a merciless crackdown on his opposition, Lukashenka became the target of sanctions from the USA. But this in turn led to greater financial aid from Russia.

2 Since the 2020 elections, Belarus and Russia have strengthened their already close ties. Minsk relies economically on its relationship with Moscow. One of their goals is to integrate their energy markets, with Russia providing supplies of natural gas to Belarus at cheaper prices than Europe would until the end of 2022. Putin has also agreed to send $630 million in loans for Alyaksandr Lukashenka's Belarus until the end of this year.

3 Russia is far and away Belarus' biggest trading partner – with 49% of the country's foreign trade being with Russia, according to the European Commission.

4 Then there's the military cooperation between the two countries. In September 2021, Russia and Belarus conducted a mass military training exercise known as Zapad-2021, which took place in some of Russia's western regions and Belarus. It lasted one week and it encompassed 15 training ranges in Russia and six in Lukashenka's territory. Around 200,000 troops, as well as planes, tanks and ships, were involved. Belarus was also used as a launchpad for part of the war in Ukraine, and Belarus has provided logistical support and air bases.

5 With Lukashenka's main support coming from Russia, it comes as no surprise that in February 2022 Lukashenka held a referendum on a new constitution for Belarus. Modelled closely on Russia's, it further cements his grip by reducing the power of parliament.

6 But is this cosying-up going to sour? While Lukashenka has defended the war, he also told The Associated Press that "this operation has dragged on".

OPPOSITE: Hanna Komar at a protest in Belarus with a sign reading "Murderers must face jail". She was detained despite protesting peacefully

been through the stages of how to deal with this comment of hers: denial, anger, depression, bargaining. So much work has been done on my side to understand her, and to never say that thing myself, to never return to the "there's-nothing-I-can-do" mindset. And I've been part of movements to stop other people in Belarus changing their mindsets. The election campaign that started in Belarus in the spring of 2020 had a huge educational element to it. The Honest People initiative, who developed a tool "Golos" (Voice) to count the real number of votes for the single alternative candidate, Sviatlana Tsikhanouskaya, encouraged Belarusians to become independent election observers, to see with their own eyes what the government was doing. But also, it encouraged us to bring the information about the real state of affairs to the traditionally pro-Lukashenka electorate, those who "didn't understand anything about politics" or believed "there was nothing we could do". We basically went and talked to our parents and grandparents, our neighbours, explaining why it was so important to vote for Tsikhanouskaya, who would enable a fair, democratic election in Belarus. We helped the older generations familiarise themselves with technology, follow independent media and use the encrypted app Telegram in order to

ABOVE: Komar continues to protest, this time in London against the war in Ukraine

receive objective information.

I talked to my mum and explained to her what was going on in the country and what we could do to improve our lives. I was certain that I did a good job, because she voted for Tsikhanouskaya, took a photo of her ballot paper and sent it to Honest People's bot, so it could be counted. A lot of things happened afterwards. I was detained and spent nine days in jail in September 2020. Mum has been worried about me many times. Every now and then she would regress to her usual ignorance – one step forward, two steps back – but once, I couldn't handle it anymore, I couldn't understand why I had to explain these things again and again, when I needed support so much.

"But what can I do?" she asked me. "Even if I am on the right side, what can I do?"

"Just believe in us, at least that, you can at least believe in us, can't you?" I almost begged her.

I knew I couldn't ask much from my mother who herself has been living under an abusive dictatorship for decades. She lost hope for a better life long ago, and she has honed her ability to shut off from the difficult reality because her survival depends on it. But I couldn't lose her to complete ignorance. I needed a mother, not a zombie.

On 2 March she shocked me again. I had neither patience nor compassion to listen to her talking about "Ukrainian Nazis attacking Russia". I ended up yelling. "Because of such stupids like you, people are dying in Ukraine!" I hung up, shaking, affected by my own anger and desperation. Then I pulled myself together and sent her recommendations on what to watch and read to understand where the truth was. She did. She apologised and told me she understood everything. "I know people are dying, but what can I do?" she asked me. "What can I do for them?"

"I just don't know who to believe," she said. In the spring of 2020, when out of the blue there appeared a number of

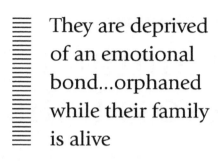

They are deprived of an emotional bond...orphaned while their family is alive

men wanting to run for president, I told a friend, "Look, I don't know who to trust," to which she replied, "Well, we definitely know who not to trust, right?"

I told my mum that knowing the truth and understanding something about politics was what she needed to do for herself. "All your life you've been told that you have to be this and you can't be that, you can't go without a man, you are incapable. But what they don't tell you on TV is that everything you have in life you've accomplished yourself, because you're strong. Don't trust the TV that tells you there's nothing you can do, trust other women and men who are doing something."

I feel proud of my mother and other parents who find inner strength to face the truth. My father, just like my friend's who I mentioned at the start, has drinking problems and is not able to perceive the harsh reality. When I was detained, his reaction was, "Well, she had it coming". I interviewed him about that episode later for my book only to find out that he was certain that I had got what I deserved because I was against the government. So I don't want to talk to him about the war and get even more distressed. And I have friends from Russia whose parents refuse to see Russia's atrocities and crimes against humanity. Both parents and their children are deprived of an emotional closeness and bond. Orphaned while their family is alive. ✖

Hanna Komar is a poet from Belarus

51(02):62/63|DOI:10.1177/03064220221110770

Culture in the cross hairs

As happened in the Soviet Union, Russia has once again singled out Ukrainian culture for attack, writes the celebrated author **ANDREY KURKOV**

AFTER FIVE DAYS of silence, my friend, a writer, journalist and historian in occupied Melitopol, finally sent me a message. I'd been afraid something had happened to her, that I would never hear from her again. But, thank God, it turned out that she'd simply had no internet access or telephone reception. I asked her to keep a diary of life under occupation, to take photos on her smartphone, and to send all that to me. I would keep it safe. The original diary could then be destroyed.

She had been living under occupation for more than two weeks and didn't set foot outside, for fear of being captured. The director of the Melitopol History Museum, Leyla Ibragimova, a Crimean Tatar, had already been kidnapped. They terrorised her, interrogated her, confiscated her and her family's phones and computers, then released her. The next morning they picked her up for another interrogation. Activists and journalists are disappearing in the occupied territories. FSB agents walk the streets with lists of names and addresses in hand. These lists were prepared before the start of the war.

Oleg Baturin, a journalist from Kakhovka, was abducted by the Russian military. Eventually, he was released - after eight days of beatings and torture, of demands to go over to the Russian side, of hunger and thirst, of humiliation. Those who beat him hid their faces and forbade him to raise his head and look at them. Is this today's Russia? Yes. But it is also the Soviet Union of the 1930s. These are the practices of the gulag. The Ukrainian author Stanislav Aseyev wrote an entire book about the torture camp in Donetsk. After two years of captivity in this camp and in the prison run by separatists, he had plenty of material. He studied closely those who beat and abused Ukrainian prisoners of war and others who had been seized on the streets and brought to this already infamous concentration camp, called "Isolation". Years ago, the place had been a factory for the manufacture of insulation for electrical wires. Later, under the same name, it became a contemporary art centre. When the separatists, aided by the Russian military, captured Donetsk, they converted it into a concentration camp, with a set of chambers in which all their detainees were tortured.

And now the same things are happening in the territories occupied by the Russian army.

We're well into 2022. Books about what is happening now in Ukraine are being written, and some have already been published.

The unsuccessful attempt to annex or, to put it plainly, occupy all of Ukraine has angered Putin and, judging by the military actions of the Russian army, Russian generals have been ordered to destroy cities and villages, to kill civilians, and simply to make sure that as much of Ukraine as possible ceases to exist.

This is not the first attempt to destroy Ukraine and Ukrainians. In the late 1920s, Ukrainian peasants refused to join collective farms, and for this the Soviet government deported 250,000 families to Siberia. In 1932-1933, as punishment for the same individualism and unwillingness to become part of Soviet collective agriculture, all reserves of wheat and, indeed, all sources of nourishment were confiscated from Ukrainian peasants, leaving them with no food for the winter. Some seven million Ukrainians perished during this artificial famine organised by Moscow.

In those same years, the Soviet government decided to destroy Ukrainian culture. Nearly all the country's leading writers, poets and playwrights were arrested, sent to Solovki in the north of Russia, and shot. In Ukrainian literary history, the

authors of this period are referred to as the "Executed Renaissance" (see p.94). These people had tried to revive Ukrainian culture after decades of official prohibitions on the use of the Ukrainian language and on anything distinctly Ukrainian in tsarist Russia. Soviet communists had decided that the revival of Ukrainian culture posed a danger to the Soviet Union. And alongside the writers, poets and playwrights they executed, the NKVD shot many artists and theatre directors. The works of Mykhaylo Semenko (1892-1937), Maik Yohansen (1895-1937), Mykola Zerov (1890-1937) and dozens of other Ukrainian writers killed in that purge could only be published again after the collapse of the USSR.

Today's Ukrainian intellectuals face the same danger. That goes for writers and journalists and historians. Anyone who believes that Ukraine should remain independent and become part of Europe is already an enemy of Russia. Culture is what cements a nation. Ukrainian culture has only just begun to revive after 70 years of Soviet rule, 70 years of censorship and persecution.

But today that culture and its representatives are the targets of Russian bombers. The attacks on Kyiv killed Artem Datsyshyn, the principal dancer of the National Opera of Ukraine, and the famed actress Oksana Shvets. Near Kyiv, in the village of Bucha - home to a number of writers and composers - Oleksandr Kislyuk, a well-known translator from Ancient Greek and other languages, a teacher at the Theological Academy, and a professor at the Drahomanov Pedagogical University, was shot by Russian soldiers on the threshold of his house. It is thanks to him that Ukrainians can read the works of Aristotle, Tacitus, Thomas Aquinas and other classic authors in their own language.

Now Oleksandr Kislyuk has been murdered and one wonders who will →

→ finish the translations he was working on in his final days.

Among those killed in this war are at least three painters. There are also photographers and scientists, musicians and architects, schoolteachers and university professors.

For several months now Russian bombers have been aiming directly at schools and universities, theatres and libraries. Near Kyiv, in the village of Ivankiv, a bomb hit a historical museum that housed the works of famous Ukrainian primitive artist Maria Prymachenko (1909-1997). While the museum burned, locals carried her paintings out of the fire. Now those canvases are kept in the homes of people who live next to the ruined museum.

The Ukrainian Ministry of Culture has sent an order to all museums to prepare their exhibits for evacuation to Western Ukraine. Some museums managed to pack up their collections, others simply lowered them into basements and underground rooms. But none have so far been evacuated. The most important thing is to evacuate people from cities under constant bombardment and artillery fire.

For two weeks, Ukrainian writers tried to extract their colleague, the Russophone prose writer Volodymyr Rafeyenko, from the village of Klavdiyevo, which was practically destroyed by the Russian army. He is a refugee twice over. First, in 2014, he had to leave his apartment in Donetsk. Since then, he and his wife had been living in Klavdiyevo, at the *dacha* of the Ukrainophone writer and translator Andriy Bondar. Klavdiyevo has been all but flattened by Russian artillery and is surrounded by their tanks. Volodymyr and his wife spent more than a week in the basement of a half-collapsed house. At long last, they managed to break out of encirclement and volunteers took them to Kyiv.

Kyiv has also been hit by rockets, but not so intensively. The chances of survival are greater in Kyiv. There, in

Now Oleksandr Kislyuk has been murdered and one wonders who will finish the translations he was working on in his final days

his apartment near the railway station, the publisher Mykola Kravchenko sits at his table and works. He's editing a novel by a young woman from Lutsk, titled Porcelain Doll. The novel concerns domestic violence. He knows that he won't be able to publish it anytime soon, but he continues to work in order to preserve his psychological balance, in order to think less about the war.

Yet the war, including the violent attack on Ukrainian cultural heritage, continues. The number of bombed-out churches is already in the tens.

The Ukrainian Ministry of Culture is still at work and every day its employees collect new information about the historical sites and cultural institutions destroyed by the Russian army.

Recently, the museum of my favourite Ukrainian philosopher and writer Grigory Skovoroda has been added to the already long list of Ukrainian cultural objects destroyed by the Russian army. It was destroyed in the village named after him, not far from Kharkiv. There were no military facilities in this village, so the destruction of the museum of Grigory Skovoroda cannot be considered an accident. Moreover, 2022 in Ukraine was declared the Year of Grigory Skovoroda. He was born in 1722 and this year, on his 300th anniversary, national celebrations were planned.

The war against Ukrainian culture has turned into a war against Ukrainian identity. In the occupied territories of Ukraine, books published in independent Ukraine after 1991 are being removed from libraries for destruction. The children of Mariupol, left orphans after the bombing of the city, are taken to Russia and given Russian passports. Schoolchildren who ended up in the occupied territories will not go on summer holidays. They will remain in schools to study the Russian language, Russian literature and Russian history. In the newly published textbooks of the history of Russia, there is no mention not only of Ukraine, but also of Kyiv and Kievan Rus.

Russia officially announced that it had taken more than one million Ukrainians from Ukraine to its territory, including about 300,000 children. They are planning to make these little Ukrainians Russians. For those deported Ukrainians who do not want to become Russians and who are now trying to leave Russia for Estonia, new filtration camps have been built on the border to prevent them from leaving in any possible way.

The Russian war has, in fact, on the contrary strengthened Ukrainian identity. And Ukrainians have begun to treat their culture even more carefully. Publishing houses in the free territory started working again, theatres opened. The Ministry of Culture announced the opening of a special bank account to raise money for the construction of a new museum of Grigory Skovoroda.

Identity cannot be killed by bombs and missiles. Probably, in Russia they do not know this. ✖

This is an updated version of an article that appeared on our website on 29 March

Andrey Kurkov is a Ukrainian author who has written 19 novels, including the bestselling Death and the Penguin

51(02):64/66|DOI:10.1177/03064220221110771

BATTLE FOR UKRAINE

Bordering on media control

Russia is trying to stir up bad blood between Poland and Ukraine. **KSENIYA TARASEVICH** talks to people in Poland about fighting these information battles

ABOVE: A temporary shelter for refugees from Ukraine in Szczenin, Poland, in March 2022. Poland is home to the largest influx of Ukrainian refugees so far

AS UKRAINIAN REFUGEES started to enter Poland, the news took a dark turn.

"During the first days of the war, around a million Poles gave shelter to Ukrainians. And suddenly, there were posts about how ungrateful Ukrainians are," said Piotr Jaworski, who is a journalist at the Polish TV station Belsat TV.

Poland and Ukraine are allies and neighbours. But they also share a complicated and at times difficult past. Historical traumas lurk beneath the surface, rising up at times like this. In 2014, for example, a Polish Facebook page emerged called "A Ukrainian is NOT my brother". It asked people to remember the Ukrainian massacres →

Traumas are being exploited by Russia, which is using fake social media profiles and pro-Russian media to provoke anti-Ukrainian sentiment

→ of Poles in the 1940s. After the latest invasion, posts have called out Polish authorities for their strong support for Ukraine.

These negative stories often link back to the Kremlin. Many believe the Facebook page is run by a woman with ties to a pro-Kremlin party, Zmiana, in Poland. Certainly traumas are being exploited by Russia, which is using fake social media profiles and pro-Russian media to provoke anti-Ukrainian sentiment.

Another false claim Polish authorities say Russians are spreading is that Poland wants to reclaim Lviv and other territory in Ukraine that once was Polish. "Those claims are untrue," the Polish Foreign Ministry said in a series of tweets. "Poland will never accept the annexation of any territory belonging to an independent state."

To complicate issues further, Poland has a long and challenging history with Russia, with memories still fresh of atrocities carried out in the 20th Century by Soviet forces. Polish journalists must also contend with attacks that come from within Poland by their own government. Media freedom has been restricted in Poland for several years now. According to the latest RSF report, Poland is ranked 66th of 180 countries in terms of media freedom. This is the worst result Poland ever received. Before the ruling party PiS came to power in 2015, Poland was ranked in 20th place.

Add all this together and you have a perfect storm when it comes to media freedom.

"We need to be attentive all the time because our government can easily

adopt new restrictive laws. That was happening all the time before the war," Violetta Szostak, journalist and editor of Gazeta Wyborcza, told Index.

The war has been used as a pretext to further close in on the media. Bartosz Zeliński, Gazeta Wyborcza's vice editor-in-chief, explains that the Polish government has closed a few pro-Russian media since it started.

"Far-right TV broadcaster wRealu24 was closed because of Russian propaganda spreading. Of course, you need to fight Russian propaganda. But we should be worried that this media was closed in a very indirect way. I am afraid that our state could do the same with the other media that the government doesn't like," he said.

Another case is that of Spanish journalist Pablo Gonzalez who was arrested on 28 February in Rzeswów, the largest city in southeast Poland. An expert in the post-Soviet world, he was working on the refugee crisis from Ukraine when Polish authorities detained him under the accusation of being a Russian agent. Despite an outcry from the International and European Federations of Journalists, Gonzalez remains in pre-trial detention at the time of going to press and faces up to 10 years in jail if convicted.

But Jaworski also says there have been positive aspects of the media story in Poland. "All in all, public opinion is saying that we need to help Ukrainians because it's the good and moral thing to do," Jaworski said.

And many stories have run on all aspects of the war, with some critical ones too in terms of the Polish government.

From the very first day, Gazeta

Wyborcza has spotlighted the war.

"We were covering almost every solidarity event that took place. Also, we featured stories of refugees. We were not silent if we saw that the governmental aid system could be improved. The other media, who are state-controlled, cannot be critical of any authorities," said Szostak.

Today Poland has the highest number of Ukrainian refugees globally and the disinformation campaign appears limited in its reach.

"We didn't even think about whether we should provide support or not," Przemek Prasnowski, the president of Barak Kultury Foundation, said. "It was something like a reflex, a quick reaction to events in Ukraine, to this tragedy that affected that many Ukrainians."

But how long can the goodwill continue? Prasnowski is afraid that the end of solidarity could be near.

"It's a tough question. Most of the volunteer work was done by simple people without financial support. The inflation rate in Poland is getting higher and higher, so people need to choose how they will spend their money".

Economic issues could potentially lead to conflict between the two nations, doctor of political philosophy Marcin Chmielowski thinks.

"Poland has limited resources, and our population grew by a few million people in a month. But there are still the same amount of houses, public transportation, schools and medical workers. There are going to be conflicts between Poles and Ukrainians, it's impossible to avoid them. A refugee got a job and a Polish citizen didn't. A Ukrainian kid got enrolled in the kindergarten and a Polish kid didn't," he told Index. ✖

Kseniya Tarasevich is a freelance journalist based in Poland

*Additional research by **Guilherme Osinski***

51(02):67/68|DOI:10.1177/03064220221110772

Treat tragedies of the Ukraine war with dignity

OLESYA KHROMEYCHUK writes about the death of her brother in Donbas, Ukraine in 2017 and the journalist's duty to not exploit someone's tragedy

AS INTELLIGENCE AGENCIES intensified their warnings about Russia's imminent attack on Ukraine, and the heads of states and governments made more visits to Kyiv in one winter than in the last three decades put together, I started to receive messages from journalists. "We are doing a piece on the potential war in Ukraine and would like to speak to you as we understand that you have a connection that would be interesting to explore." Variations of this request arrived with increased frequency.

Hearing of the "potential war" made me despair even before I had the chance to reply. "The war began in 2014. If you are aware of my "connection" then you will know that for me - as for the rest of the country - this war has been going on for years. It's not

about to begin." I drafted variations of this response but deleted them before replying: "Yes, of course. I'll be happy to speak to you."

My "connection" is my brother. Volodya, forever 42. Forever living in my heart. The heart that broke in 2017 when Volodya's heart stopped beating. By 2022, I thought I had mostly dealt with my grief. I squeezed the bleeding memories of my brother out of my mind as I was writing a book about Volodya's death. Once the book was finished, I felt it was time for my grief to take on a different form, a passive sort that no longer wakes you up in the night as you re-live the horror of realisation that he is really gone.

My grief was maturing with me. Five years after his death, I'm five years closer in age to my brother. In four more years, I'll catch up with him and begin to overtake him in age. I thought as I read those emails from the journalists that now was the time to use my mature grief as a tool to tell the world what sorrow Russia's aggression has already caused in Ukraine so that the world can prevent it from escalating.

"You have a brother in Ukraine, right?"

"I... had a brother. Yes." I never know what tense to use in these situations.

"A soldier, right?"

"Yes, he ... was a soldier. Well, no, he wasn't really. He was an artist; he was many things. But he joined the army in 2015 and volunteered to fight in Donbas."

> ## Hearing of the "potential war" made me despair – this war has been going on for years

LEFT & INSET: Olesya Khromeychuk, from Ukraine, is a historian, writer and the author of A Loss: The story of a dead soldier told by his sister

I can sense the journalist getting impatient at the other end of the line. They don't want to know my family history. They want to see if my "connection" will work for their "story". So, I cut my story short.

"He was killed at the frontline in 2017. You see, many people have already died in this war. It's really important that Putin is stopped before many more die."

"Oh, I'm so sorry to hear that" some of them say in response. Others don't bother. "But I'm not sure we'll be able to use this for our report/article/ programme. It's not quite the right fit for what we have in mind. Don't suppose you know someone who's in danger now; perhaps living close to the frontline and is afraid that Russia might attack? Maybe someone who's serving in the army now?"

"Let me think about it and get back to you," I reply and feel the familiar pain in my chest. Turns out that the ageing grief can cause as much trouble as the young.

A couple of weeks later, after 24 February, over 40 million people found themselves in danger. The journalists must feel spoiled for choice. So many are the right fit. So many broken connections have become news stories.

As the pain of loss is turned into reporting, let's consume it with care. It is sometimes all that the grieving hearts have left of their loved ones.

Olesya Khromeychuk is the director of the Ukrainian Institute London, a historian and author of 'Undetermined' Ukrainians (2013) and A Loss (2021)

51(02):69/69|DOI:10.1177/03064220221110773

Worth a gamble

An organisation helping Russians receive accurate information
on the Ukraine war finds unlikely allies in those running
Russia's gambling sites, writes **JEMIMAH STEINFELD**

THERE IS ONE silver lining to rampant corruption in Russia – with a little bit of money many people will turn against the law. Of course that's bad when the law is there to protect people, but it's good when the law is something aimed at silencing the population, as is the case of Russia's new "fake news" law. This law, passed shortly after the invasion of Ukraine, makes any honest criticism of the war a punishable crime. Even calling it a war (Russian President Vladimir Putin would rather go with "special operation") can land people in jail.

It's because of the corruptible nature of Russian web entrepreneurs that an organisation working with Index has been able to flood the Russian internet with adverts linking to independent news about the war in Ukraine. There's no magic formula here. They've simply paid people in Russia operating myriad websites to replace their typical ads selling products like cars or trainers with ads linking to the un-airbrushed truth about the war in Ukraine. The hope is people will read this independent news, share it with friends and family and seek out more news of a similar nature.

"From Putin's perspective we are a criminal spam operation," said Rob Blackie, one of the organisation's directors.

He told Index that to date their ads have been seen 283 million times by at least five million people. They either show direct news or, when that's not possible, they use a cover ad to direct people to where they can access the news (often on a dummy site). A quarter of a million people have already clicked through to these articles.

Informally called "Free Russia", Blackie works as part of a team of four, with approximately 60 people volunteering to help. Many of those in their network are Russian-speaking Ukrainians, a chunk of whom work at marketing agencies and just want to help the war effort.

The idea behind the organisation was first trialled by Blackie eight years ago, also in Russia and also to great success.

Even though the idea is simple, the execution is far from it, another weapon in their arsenal. Digital advertising is a logistical minefield. It's "remarkably complex" said Blackie, who himself has a background in both corporate digital advertising and political campaigning.

"Very few people understand all of it. That means censorship of digital advertising is really hard," he added.

He said Russia doesn't have the government capacity to regulate and control all advertising online and that "fundamentally it's so corrupt that organisations aren't really used to thinking about how to follow the law".

Blackie cannot reveal the companies they buy the ad space from. Despite

From Putin's perspective we are a criminal spam operation

 People who have done the least ethical stuff are the best for us. They know the devious ways to get around the law

probing him several times about whether these hard-hitting ads had found themselves on, say, gambling and pornographic sites, he kept schtum. He did say though that some of their "most useful volunteers have been ones who have worked on gambling sites before."

"People who have done the least ethical stuff are the most valuable to us. They know the devious ways of how to crack these systems."

Whatever they are doing is clearly working well when it comes to Russia's censors as, in addition to their ads being seen a lot, they have "never been fundamentally banned" (they've always been able to get back on a site).

So is this the new frontier to fight oppression? Alexey Navalny, the currently jailed opponent of Vladimir Putin, has called for just this sort of campaign. And Blackie says that they have recently received a large amount of funding, which will keep them in business for the foreseable future.

Free Russia is also operating in Belarus, a country which Russia sees as a potential source of recruits too. They're placing ads to make said people think twice. Beyond this region, Blackie has done a research trip to China. Maybe the Great Firewall is the next one to crack? ✖

Jemimah Steinfeld is editor-in-chief at Index

51(02):70/71|DOI:10.1177/03064220221110774

COMMENT

"The power of art is in our shared humanity and not in division"

MARIA SORENSEN, FROM BELARUS, ON WHY SHE DOESN'T FEEL HER NATIONALITY AND THE
COUNTRY'S ARTISTS EQUALS LUKASHENKA | CANCEL PUTIN, NOT CULTURE, P.92

BATTLE FOR UKRAINE | DEBATE: CANCEL RUSSIAN CULTURE?

Cancelling Russian culture is today's moral imperative

Putin has used Russian culture to further his aims. Promoting it today
risks furthering his agenda, writes **MARINA PESENTI**

SINCE THE WAR started, Ukraine
has become a magnet for the
global media. As the war has
progressed, its voice has become
stronger in cultural matters, too.
Ukraine has emerged from the shadows
of its murderous "brother" and thrust
itself into the western imagination,
bleeding, yet stoic, full of raw emotion.
It stopped being "the Ukraine". "Kiev"
became "Kyiv."

Western intellectuals and the public
suddenly started browsing Wikipedia
pages on Ukraine's history, trying to
dissect reasons for its obstinance in the
face of the enemy.

The Russia-Ukraine war has many
layers. It's a war of democracy versus
authoritarianism. It is a war of blatant
propaganda versus principled journalism.
It is also a classical colonial war of a
metropolis against one of its former

subjects. A liberation struggle, extending
into the realm of history and culture.

There's a growing consensus among
Ukraine's cultural elites that this war
should become a point of no-return
for Russia trying to impose its imperial
blueprint on the perception of history
and culture of this region, both
domestically and internationally.

In the early days of the war, as the
first Russian rockets hit the Ukrainian

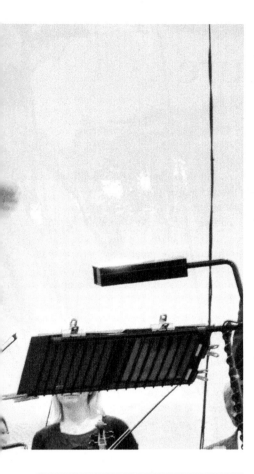

ABOVE: Valery Gergiev with the London Symphony Orchestra. His relationship with Putin has seen him being dropped for performances

capital, Ukrainian Institute, a young state institution with a mandate to promote Ukraine's standing in the world through cultural diplomacy instruments, published a manifesto, calling on international partners to stop cooperation with Russia's state cultural institutions. Similar to weaning itself off Russian energy, the West needs to stop thoughtlessly consuming Russian cultural products, without contextualising them, the Institute said.

As Russian artillery pound Ukrainian cities, London's leading museums continue feeding the narrative about great Russian culture and history to their audiences. "Fabergé in London: Romance to Revolution"opened at the V&A shortly before the invasion. It

profiles "craftsmanship and luxury" of Carl Fabergé, the jeweller of the Russian imperial family. The backdrop of the story is Russia's imperial history and close ties between both monarchies.

There has since been a pivot. British museums are suddenly showing more willingness towards giving Ukraine agency. London's National Gallery reviewed its stance on a Degas canvas in its permanent collection, depicting a swirl of dancers in a distinctly Ukrainian traditional attire. "Russian Dancers" became "Ukrainian Dancers". Tate Modern is currently working on a new exhibition project with Ukraine as its focus, the first of its kind in its history.

Ukraine's cultural elites and scholars worldwide are determined to seize this moment and to shift the paradigm where imperial hierarchies persist. As it has stood the histories of big countries, mostly former empires, and their cultural figures and phenomena matter more than those of their colonial subjects. This explains why there are so few centres for Ukrainian Studies in the UK (Cambridge being the notable exception), so few translations of Ukrainian literature. No exhibitions in major museums, up until now.

"We cannot cancel Russian culture." "Pushkin cannot be held responsible for Putin." "We cannot exclude Russian artists from being invited to residencies and collaborative projects." "It's illiberal." "It smacks of censorship." These are the arguments often deployed by many intellectuals and creatives in the West. Let us address these concerns one by one.

Placing Russia at the centre of any cultural conversation should not happen without clear articulation of the fact that Russia has used culture for the purposes of aggressive political propaganda internationally. Culture is a broad reflection of the society it represents, and currently Russian society stands largely united behind an ideology promoting violence and blatant untruths.

The new consensus should go beyond the outcome of the Ukraine-Russia conflict and should be about realisation that cultural discourse is unfairly skewed in favour of big and powerful countries, denying many voice and agency. And Ukraine is not alone here.

Our perception of one's culture is often shaped by a sheer fact of its presence on the cultural scene: through books, theatre productions, films and exhibitions. We often forget that there's a powerful state machinery propping up this presence and that rogue states – and Russia has become one – weaponise culture and history to political ends, and even use them as a pretext to start a war. To be remembered, the Russian intent behind the killings in Ukraine is to "de-Nazify" the country.

Artists and academics often lack a toolkit to study and bring to the fore cultures previously absent from the discourse. These cultures are absent or underrepresented not for the reasons of uninteresting or lacking value. They are absent because of entrenched cultural hierarchies, intellectual laziness, lack of courage to work with original sources, as well as a long history of suppression of their culture and language by the metropolis.

It is intellectually dishonest and arrogant to place Ukrainian and "good" Russian artists on the same footing by inviting them to speak at the same panel discussion or to apply for funding, for the sake of "reconciliation" and "dialogue". There can be no reconciliation while the war is still on. It can only start happening after Russia has admitted its guilt and paid reparations for the damage done. Any other framework would mean perpetuation of the colonial discourse. ✖

Marina Pesenti is a member of the Supervisory Board of Ukrainian Institute. She researches and writes on soft power, culture and media

51(02):74/75|DOI:10.1177/03064220221110775

Cancel Putin, not culture

MARIA SORENSEN calls for artists to unite in their opposition to authoritarian regimes and an end to the blanket boycott of Russian culture

In the dark times
Will there be singing?
Yes, there will be singing
About the dark times.

Bertolt Brecht, motto to Svendborg Poems 1939

For someone who has by now lived most of my adult life in the West but grew up in Belarus – a country that borders both Ukraine and Russia – these have certainly been dark and turbulent times.

The horror of what people in Ukraine are going through is heart-breaking. It is also confusing if my own country of birth is viewed as an aggressor or a victim.

Should people who have bravely protested in hundreds of thousands in 2020 and paid a very high price for it be now equated to the regime that rules them? Does Belarus, the country and the people, mean Lukashenka? What about Russia? The support for Putin is undoubtedly bigger there. But does Russia and Russian culture mean Putin?

Having always been a passionate advocate of freedom of expression under the most trying of conditions, what to make now of the blanket censorship of Russian and Belarusian artists not in Russia and Belarus… but in the West?

When the horror of the invasion of 24 February sank in, the Western cultural scene was immediately rocked by a succession of cancellations and calls for boycotts. Some of them were easier to understand and justify than others.

Opera singer Anna Netrebko and conductor Valery Gergiev have been tied to Putin's regime and identified as representatives of his soft power:

association with them became too toxic for Western cultural institutions. Recently, the evidence of oligarchic wealth accumulated by Gergiev due to his political connections has also come to light. This made any defence of him even more difficult

Art in some ways has always been held hostage. The authoritarian Soviet regime used the prestige of the Bolshoi and the power of Russian culture as soft power.

One is reminded of a powerful 1968 performance by cellist Mstislav Rostropovich at the BBC Proms in London where he performed - intitally to the calls of protest and with tears streaming down his face - a tortured and impassioned piece of music by a Czech composer Antonin Dvorak on the day Soviet tanks rolled into Czechoslovakia to crush the Prague Spring.

His wife, the opera singer Galina Vishnevskaya, recalled the event in her autobiography:

"In the hall, six thousand people greeted the appearance of Soviet artists with long unceasing cries, stomping, whistling, preventing the concert from starting. Some shouted: 'Soviet fascists, get out!' Others: 'Shut up, the artists are not to blame!'

"Slava (his nickname) stood there completely pale, absorbing the shame for his criminal government, and I, closing my eyes and not daring to raise my head, huddled in the far corner of the viewing

box. But then, finally, the hall fell silent. Dvořák's music poured over the people like a requiem, and Rostropovich, shedding tears, spoke through his cello.

"The hall froze, listening to the confession of the great artist, who at that moment, together with Dvořák merged with the very soul of the Czech people, suffering with him and with them asking his forgiveness and praying for them.

"As soon as the last note played, I rushed backstage to Slava. Pale, with trembling lips, having not yet recovered from his experience on stage, with eyes full of tears, he grabbed my arm and dragged me to the exit:

"'Let's go to the hotel, I can't see anyone.'

"We went out into the street - the demonstrators were shouting there, waiting for the musicians of the orchestra to express their indignation to them.

"Seeing the two of us, they suddenly fell silent and parted in front of us. In the ensuing silence, not looking at anyone, feeling like criminals, we quickly walked to the car waiting for us and, returning to the hotel, we could finally give vent to our despair.

"But what could we do? We did the only thing that was in our power - got drunk."

What then should the answer to this moral dilemma be? Should musicians and artists be allowed to perform only once they have stated their opposition to their government?

 We need to ask ourselves who ultimately benefits from silencing?

RIGHT: The cast of the world famous Bolshoi Ballet rehearsing at the Royal Opera House in London. Despite the war, many intellectuals believe the world shouldn't cancel or stop consuming Russia's culture

And is it then morally justifiable from the point of view of Western democracies to put someone living under completely different conditions in that position? To demand dissent from someone who might not be in the position to speak freely?

The German music critic Jan Brachmann gives the example of Dmitri Shostakovich, who, in 1949, appeared at a Soviet-backed peace conference in New York, having been pressured by Stalin into attending.

The émigré Russian composer Nicolas Nabokov publicly interrogated Shostakovich about Soviet denunciations of modernist music, even though he knew that his colleague could not speak his mind. Shostakovich muttered, barely audible: "I fully agree with the statements made in Pravda."

It is unclear what exactly had been gained from that exercise. But Gurgiev aside and any moral clarity there notwithstanding, there have been other, much less clear-cut cases recently.

Sergei Loznitsa, one of Ukraine's most prolific filmmakers, who has explored the Maidan uprising, the Donbass war, Stalin's personality cult and the tragedy behind the Babyn Yar massacre, has recently been expelled from the Ukrainian Film Academy for speaking out against blanket boycott of Russian filmmakers.

His opposition is based on the fact that people should be judged by their actions not their passports. It is hard to disagree. People can still love their country and feel deeply ashamed of their government's actions.

Kirill Serebrennikov, a Russian dissenting artist of great talent, is currently also in the line of fire. Serebrennikov, who had his homoerotic production, Nureyev, taken off stage

at Bolshoi in 2017, was placed under house arrest accused of embezzling theatre funds – a charge widely seen as being politically motivated. He was not allowed to attend a premiere of his production of Cosi Fan Tutte at Zurich Opera nor to the Cannes premiere of his hugely acclaimed ode to rock 'n' roll and dissent in 1980s Leningrad, Leto.

Recently Bolshoi has once again cancelled a scheduled production of Nureyev, this time as a retaliation for him speaking up against the war. Serebrennikov told France 24 in an interview last month that "it's quite obvious that Russia started the war", and that it was breaking his heart.

"It's war, it's killing people, it's the worst thing (that) ever might happen with civilisation, with mankind... It's a humanitarian catastrophe, it's rivers of blood," he said.

And yet the Ukrainian State Film Agency opposed Serebrennikov's inclusion in Cannes Film Festival and the premiere of his new film on the grounds that he is a Russian filmmaker, and it was unacceptable in times of war. While this reaction is humanly understandable and can even be seen by some as a moral decision, we need to ask ourselves

who ultimately benefits from silencing, cancelling, de-platforming and similar methods? It is never a viewer, a reader or any ordinary person.

The power of art is in our shared humanity and not in division. Art and its healing power is what gets us through the hard and dark times. We need to show solidarity with people in Ukraine and Ukrainian artists, shine a spotlight on their experiences and prioritise their voices, as well as support those who struggle under authoritarianism in their own countries. This is a task for any functioning democracy.

Having started by quoting Bertolt Brecht, another quotation, this time by the Soviet dissident Alexander Solzhenitsyn comes to mind: "The line separating good and evil passes not through states, nor between classes, nor between political parties either – but right through every human heart – and through all human hearts." ✖

Maria Sorensen is a Belarusian writer based in Switzerland. She runs the Art Against Aggression Facebook group

51(02):76/77|DOI:10.1177/03064220221110776

Beware the 'civilisation' battle

Criticise Russia by all means, but leave racism out of it, writes **EMILY COUCH**

ABOVE: Vladimir Putin meets French President Emmanuel Macron in Moscow, in February 2022

WHEN RUSSIAN PRESIDENT Vladimir Putin launched a full-scale invasion of Ukraine, Western governments were quick to rally behind Kyiv and cast Russia as being definitively on the wrong side of history. This is all to be expected in a war where there is a clear aggressor and a clear victim. There is, however, a troubling strand to such rhetoric: the attribution of Russia's aggression to its "Asian-ness".

First, some examples. Canadian political analyst Michael MacKay tweeted in April: "Russia's invasion of Ukraine is part of its war against Western civilisation ... Culturally, historically, politically – Ukraine is the West. Russia is a Eurasian country, mostly in Asia. Muscovy never has been of the West." Dirk Mattheisen, former assistant corporate secretary of the World Bank Group, has attributed Russia's "tendency towards authoritarianism" to "the straight line from Mongol vassal, to Mongol agent, to oppressor, to empire, to autocratic (and predatory) socialism, to Putin's national democracy". In the wake of the invasion, Florence Gaub, deputy director of the EU Institute for Security Studies, posted a Twitter thread responding to the war, arguing that Russia was fundamentally Asian rather than European.

This rhetorical trope has not been the preserve of Western analysts. Erica Marat, associate professor of regional and analytical studies at the National Defence University, noted: "Russian intellectuals routinely blame Mongol and Tatar rule on Russia's territory for contemporary authoritarianism in Russia."

The following tweet by prominent Russian independent journalist Yulia

These ideas perpetuate racist stereotypes and disregard the cultural sophistication of the Mongol Empire

Latynina exemplifies this. "We are witnessing the rebirth of the Kievan Rus. Everything democratic, market-oriented and Western will be concentrated in Kyiv. Kyiv will once more become the capital of the Rus. Moscow will be the capital of the horde."

Marat explains the popularity of this rhetoric, stating that "unchallenged stereotypes against Asians … help Russians (*russkiye* [ethnic Russians] not *rossiyaniye* [citizens of the Russian Federation regardless of ethnicity]) maintain a sense of cultural superiority and innocence even in the face of genocidal war."

These examples are by no means exhaustive, but they are indicative of the disturbing undercurrent present in liberal perceptions of the war.

The notion that Asian people are inherently violent and "uncivilised" is nothing new. One need only look to the justifications for Western imperialist projects penned over the last several centuries to see that.

In an interview with Index, Kate Antonova, associate professor of history at the City University of New York, expands on this historical pattern, saying: "That image goes back at least to the foreigner accounts of Ivan the Terrible's court in the 16th century. It was created then, and maintained for centuries, by Britain, which lived in constant dread of Russian incursions on their trade empire, though this threat never materialised. After Europe nearly destroyed itself in two world wars … Americans took on the lore."

Edward Said addresses the construction of the "Orient" as a repository for Western fears and fantasies about physical and sexual violence in his influential book Orientalism.

Whether Russia is Asian or European has long been an intensely debated question. Arguments that it is the former take as a starting point the conquering of the Kievan Rus by the Mongol Empire – known as the Golden Horde – in the 13th century. The term

Relegating Russia to this constructed and highly problematic conception eases the path for anti-democratic actors

"horde" has since become a byword for barbarism and military might. Not only do these ideas perpetuate racist stereotypes and disregard the cultural sophistication of the Mongol Empire they also do an immense disservice to the vibrant democracies that currently exist on the continent.

Testament to the absurdity of attributing Russia's authoritarianism to Mongol influence is that Mongolia ranks as "free" in Freedom House's Freedom in the World index with a score of 84/100. Russia's score is just 19.

Even those who believe the opposite – that Russia is an essentially European nation held back by authoritarian and kleptocratic governance – implicitly buy into the conception of "European-ness" equaling democracy and civilisation while "Asian-ness" equals despotism and barbarism.

Relegating Russia to this constructed and highly problematic conception eases the path for anti-democratic actors within Western countries. By essentialising authoritarianism – casting it as a phenomenon that is inherent to certain countries and not to others – we refuse to turn our gaze towards the erosion of democracy occurring at home.

Moreover, the false binary between "barbaric Asian Russia" and the "civilised European West" obscures the latter's history of imperial violence.

Attributing Russia's war against Ukraine to this constructed notion will not aid the latter's victory; nor will it help us to understand the former's motivations for its horrific onslaught.

On the contrary, it plays into the hands of the Kremlin propagandists who seek, in their own way, to present Russia as besieged on all sides in a civilisational battle. It also obfuscates the

not-insignificant responsibility borne by Western countries for enabling the war by looking the other way to Putin's earlier aggressions, and for the anti-democratic tendencies within their own societies.

Russia's war against Ukraine is not a clash between Western and Asian civilisations. It has nothing to do with the country's geographic location or historical connection with the Mongol Empire, but everything to do with the expansionist policies and ideologies of cultural superiority – similar to those of Western imperial projects – pursued by successive Russian regimes.

Only by understanding this can we stand as true allies to Ukraine. ✖

Emily Couch is contributing editor (Ukraine and Russia) of Index on Censorship

51(02):78/79|DOI:10.1177/03064220221110777

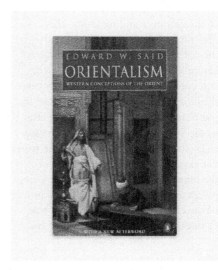

ABOVE: Edward Said's important work Orientalism, which looks at how the "Orient" was constructed as a repository for Western fears and fantasies

The silent minority

Reflecting on the origins of Index, **RUTH SMEETH** pays tribute to the writers and artists whose work never saw the light of day

N MAY, I had the privilege of spending some time with the founding editor of Index on Censorship magazine, Michael Scammell. It was a joy to learn more about our history from the first member of professional staff – the man who shaped our organisation, defined our priorities as a voice for the persecuted and led the fight for freedom of expression as a liberal democratic value.

Michael was on the frontline during some of the most era-defining moments of the Cold War era and it was because of him – and the efforts of our founding trustees, Stephen Spender, David Astor, Elisabeth Longford, Stuart Hampshire and Peter Calvocoressi – that Index launched a magazine and has since led the campaign for freedom of expression around the globe.

As Michael reminisced about the challenges of founding Index, the difficulties in securing content and the realities of supporting *samizdat* activities, I was struck by one off-the-cuff comment. He stated that only one third of the work that was intended for publication by Index – or anyone else in the West for that matter – managed to be sneaked out from behind the Iron Curtain. That's only one in three of the manuscripts, the artwork, the news pieces and the analysis. Given the power of the censors, the extended network of internal and external spies and the

border forces, I know we should be amazed that even a third of the work by our fellow writers, scholars and artists got out and was published and displayed in the West. That achievement alone was miraculous.

But I keep thinking about the material, the words and the art that never made it. The plays which were ripped up by customs agents, the novels that were thrown away by the police, the artwork that was destroyed or damaged as people had to abandon efforts to "liberate" it, the first-hand accounts of the acts of repression which were added to KGB files but never saw the light of day.

We don't know what we have lost, and I can't help thinking about what could have been.

What masterpieces did the world never get to see? What intellectual arguments did we never get to hear because the papers were destroyed en route to the West? Whose names should we know, but we never learned because the evidence of their genius was destroyed or they were imprisoned? And just as importantly, what level of despair did our allies and comrades reach when they realised that their work wasn't going to be seen and that their efforts at quiet rebellion and defiance had failed at the first hurdle? I can only imagine the emotional rollercoaster as brave dissidents invested their hearts and souls in these works – only to learn that they hadn't reached their intended audience. Even worse than that was the fear that their work may have reached an agent of the state and concerns about what could happen next to them and their families.

What masterpieces did the world never get to see?

ABOVE: Russian samizdat from the USSR. What important literature and stories never managed to make it across the border?

Living with this fear every day, knowing that your family and colleagues are at risk of paying the ultimate price because of your values, your art, your words and your actions must truly be all-consuming. Guilt, fear, righteous anger and the determination to make a stand – that really is an emotional rollercoaster and one that we are seeing replicated in Russia and Belarus today.

In the face of unbelievable aggression in Ukraine and the curtailment of basic human rights in Russia, many of the intelligentsia have fled in order to protect their lives. But many more have made the decision to stay – either because they can't leave or because they don't want to. Many of those who remain seem to be

trying to find a way to make their home a better place, to make it clear that they do not stand with Vladimir Putin and his aggression and that they seek to live in a peaceful, progressive society. These people are risking their lives to send a message to Putin and his acolytes – just as their predecessors did at the height of the Cold War.

In the first 100 days of the Russian invasion of Ukraine, 15,445 Russians were detained for protesting the war. Journalists have made every effort, in the most hostile of environments, to shine a light on events both in Ukraine and in Russia and have been arrested and fined for their efforts. Artists are using their skills to spread the word through guerrilla art tactics in supermarkets and on the streets to highlight what is really happening in Ukraine and how many Russian soldiers and sailors are dying.

These people are our inspiration. Index, of course, stands with the people of Ukraine. We stand against tyranny and we stand for our shared fundamental human rights, the most central of which is the right to live free of fear and persecution – a basic right no longer afforded to the people of Ukraine, a population which lives in daily fear of bombardment, destruction, war crimes and death. Our hearts bleed for them and Index will do everything in our power to support them.

But we cannot forget that those basic human rights, which we hold so dear, are also not available to the overwhelming majority of the Russian and Belarusian people. Any sign of dissent is squashed and, as we have seen with Putin's brutal treatment of Alexey Navalny, punishment for any form of opposition could be attempted

assassination or, worse still, death.

This magazine was launched by Michael Scammell to provide a platform for those people who demanded more from their governments, who aspired to a world where words were cherished and intellect rewarded. A world where leaders acted in the interests of their citizens and where the liberal democratic value of freedom of expression was the lynchpin to securing the rest of our fundamental human rights. It is in this tradition that Index seeks to operate today in Ukraine, in Russia, in Belarus, in China, in India and in many other countries. In 1972, Index was created to be a voice for the persecuted. In 2022 that remains our sole objective. ✖

Ruth Smeeth is CEO of Index on Censorship

51(02):80/81|DOI:10.1177/03064220221110778

OUTSOURCING REPRESSION

EVERYDAY
STATE POWER
IN
CONTEMPORARY
CHINA

LYNETTE H. ONG

CULTURE

"Their writing was naturally radical, because to write in Ukrainian
was, by definition, to oppose imperial orthodoxy and colonisation"

STEPHEN KOMARNYCKYJ INTRODUCES THE UKRAINIAN POETS THAT THE USSR DID NOT WANT ANYONE TO READ | POETIC INJUSTICE, P.94

'The light is no longer the light it used to be'

LYUBA YAKIMCHUK spoke to **STEPHEN KOMARNYCKYJ** and **JEMIMAH STEINFELD** about years of oppression in Donbas and war's effect on words. Plus one of her poems printed here

THE PRAYER-LIKE WORDS of Lyuba Yakimchuk may be what this year's Grammy Awards will be best known for. "Forgive us our destroyed cities, even though we do not forgive … our enemies," she said as she implored listeners to protect her family and her country.

A name few outside Ukraine had heard of until that moment, Yakimchuk, 36, has long been a prominent voice within Ukraine's literary circles, and in 2015 she was listed in the 100 most influential cultural figures by Kyiv's New Time magazine.

War is not new to Yakimchuk. If anything, it's defined much of her career. Originally from the Donbas region, she was visiting her parents at their family home in 2014 when the area was invaded by Russian troops. Witnessing the conflict, and seeing friends killed and imprisoned, influenced her book of poems, Apricots of Donbas. We publish one of them below and discuss with Yamichuk the implications of Russia's war when it comes to freedom in Ukraine.

INDEX ON CENSORSHIP Let's begin with your book. Why was it called Apricots of Donbas? What does the book have to tell an English audience about Ukraine?

LYUBA YAKIMCHUK The motto to the poem of the same name which begins the book runs as follows: "Where no more apricots grow, Russia starts."

However much Ukrainian territory Russians occupy, the planting of apricots – which are on our side of the eastern border and disappear when you cross over the border post – continues to flourish although, of course, trees are destroyed by explosions and traces of chemicals left by missiles poison the soil.

The apricot trees nevertheless continue to grow, flourish and bear fruit throughout these eight years of war in east Ukraine because, unsurprisingly, apricot trees are more stable than real borders. That's why I selected apricots as a marker of Ukrainian and non-Ukrainian territory.

The book itself is about the difference between love in a country where there is war and love in a country where there is no war: about the elusive meanings of words that change simply during our lives and, therefore, the elusive feelings that we name with these words. It also concerns what happens to a country and its people when the war begins. It shows how, during a war, poetry in its old meaning is impossible, and only the decomposition of forms and meanings is possible, because literature competes with reality and loses out to it. Military reality is always more impressive than literature, whereas in a peaceful country the opposite is true. I'm searching for ways to speak about military losses.

IOC What is the situation with freedom of speech in the fake "republics" that Russia has created in the occupied Donetsk People's Republic (DPR) and the Luhansk People's Republic (LPR)?

LY Russia continues its imperial, colonial policy toward Ukraine, which it has pursued since the days of the Russian Empire and, subsequently, the Soviet Union. This comprises oppression of Ukrainian culture, banning the Ukrainian language or treating it as underdeveloped, and suppressing freedom of expression by all measures and means, including torture. Over the last few centuries, Russian discourse on Ukrainians, whom they regard as an inferior category of Russian, and concerning the Ukrainian language, which they consider a ridiculous dialect, has been consistently imperial and aggressive. The consequences of this policy are most pronounced in the so-called LPR and DPR, and in the

LEFT: Ukrainian poet Lyuba Yakimchuk performs onstage during the 2022 Annual Grammy Awards

territories occupied by Russia in south and east Ukraine this year.

Initially, after establishing their power upon gaining control over these territories, the Russian occupiers confiscated textbooks on history and Ukrainian literature, both modern and classical. The situation is different across these locations: in some places they are just removed, in other areas they burn them.

Independent journalists and bloggers are arrested and charged with sabotage or terrorism. In the DPR there is a special concentration camp in the premises of the former arts centre Izolyatsia ("Isolation"). Exhibitions were once held there, poets gave readings, but now people or journalists who criticise the occupiers or simply express their Ukrainian viewpoint are tortured and abducted and interned in this location. Incidentally, you can read in detail about this camp in a book by Stanislav Aseyev, The Torture Camp on Paradise Street, which has been translated into English. He escaped from that torture chamber thanks to a prisoner exchange.

You can be criminally liable now for public criticism of these so-called "republics", including for "slander" on social networks. (My understanding is that this law is copied from Russian legislation.)

If in Russia, prior to 24 February, there were still some free media that called things by their correct names (they are closed down now), in the so-called LPR and DPR they did not exist, and they either tortured or got rid of all the independent journalists.

Freedom of expression isn't even mentioned during hostilities. Many people from Mariupol pass through Russian filtration camps: their phones are checked, their correspondence is read, they are undressed, inspected and searched for tattoos with inscriptions or symbols. Anything that the Russians do not like can lead to a person's murder – although sometimes they don't need a specific reason for their antipathy. In the first week of the war, for example, there was an order to kill people in black clothing.

IOC Russia says that it is "de-Nazifying" Ukraine, but reading the articles in the Russian media anything Ukrainian seems to be Nazi. Do you know what is happening in terms of education, literature and censorship in the occupied areas?

LY If we talk about the Nazis in Ukraine, they are here, they are the Russian occupiers. All the Nazis I've seen can't pronounce the word *polânicâ* and have Russian passports. Some of them left Ukraine with looted refrigerators, microwaves, sneakers and even underwear, transporting them on tanks to Belarus or Russia.

With regard to education, they took Russian programmes as a basis and developed a separate course on the history of the "People of Donbas" which contains elements of indoctrination – in particular the attitude to Ukraine as occupying the LPR or the DPR. This is nonsense! In short, they are brainwashing children with some fictitious historians working on their policies of invasion.

IOC In terms of misinformation, what are you most concerned about?

LY All Ukrainian media are silenced in the occupied territories and Russian TV is exclusively broadcast there. It contains a large amount of misinformation, as well as staged news, which is created with the participation of actors, and even occasionally scenery, and often not even in Ukraine. Russians present reality in a distorted and very emotional way. This disorients people, especially the elderly. If you do not have access to other sources of information, you begin to live in this fictional, hysterical world.

IOC In 2017 you produced a film along with Taras Tomenko focused on →

ABOVE: People hide in an official underground shelter in Lviv, Ukraine, after the beginning of Russia's invasion

All the Nazis I've seen can't pronounce the word polânicâ and have Russian passports

→ The Executed Renaissance – that generation of Ukrainian writers who rose in the 1920s only to be destroyed by the Russian regime of the 1930s. The film, however, emphasised that they were ultimately triumphant and renamed them The Undestroyed Renaissance.

IOC Do you see any parallels between the events taking place now and that period which included the Holodomor [an artificial famine targeting Ukraine] and the mass executions of the Ukrainian intelligentsia?

LY I see this as, above all, consisting of new attempts to subdue Ukrainians and exterminate those who cannot be subdued. You mentioned the Holodomor, which was artificially created in Ukraine by the Moscow authorities, so I'll tell you of a recent episode in the conflict. The legislative assembly of the Krasnoyarsk Territory decided to conduct an "expropriation of surplus Ukrainian harvest" in the Kherson region as part of the "special operation". They published this decision on their website without a moment's thought and then deleted it.

Russian troops in the newly occupied Ukrainian territories are currently seizing grain and oil – sending a portion to Russia, and trying to sell a portion on foreign markets. Even as we speak, a Russian ship with stolen Ukrainian grain, which a port in Alexandria refused to accept, is roaming the sea somewhere.

If you look at the terminology used

I have a crisis for you

you lit up a cigarette
but it wouldn't burn
it was summer
and girls would light up from any passer-by
but I didn't light up from you anymore

—our love's gone missing, I explain to a friend
it vanished in one of the wars
we waged in our kitchen
—change the word 'war' to 'crisis,' he suggests
because a crisis is something everyone has from time to time

remember the Second World Crisis?
correspondingly, also the First World
Civil Crisis—to each his own
I forgot about the Cold Crisis
it seems they also came in twos
also the Uprising Crisis
it sounds so good—
the Uprising Crisis of 1648–1657
write it down in the textbooks
a crisis that liberates
releases forever

my great-grandfather fell in the Second World Crisis
possibly by the hand of my other great-grandfather
or his machine gun
or his battle tank
but it is unclear
how they conducted this crisis with each other

in such documents, all of these words, such as the "expropriation of surpluses", are words taken from the Moscow decrees that led to the Holodomor. The Russians also want to achieve famine conditions now. Ukrainians are already starving during the occupation and there is simultaneously a threat of starvation in African countries which Ukraine supplies with grain.

IOC Please do tell us about your poem at the Grammys and the experience.

We can only imagine that it must have felt bittersweet, performing at such a high-profile event, but under such awful circumstances.

LY Yes, it was a two-sided emotion. I went from the war to the Grammys. I was under enormous stress, and slept no more than four to five hours a day. I went and checked the news 10 times daily. It was terrifying. I was worried about my partner, who was transporting humanitarian aid to Kharkiv, where

perhaps it was the crisis itself that killed them, like a plague
for nobody is to blame for the crisis
it is inexorable like death

and when our own domestic war
turns into crisis
does it get better?
does it hurt less?
do birds come back to us from the south
or maybe, we come out to meet them?
why is our language like that—
we lack words to describe our feelings
only crisis and love are left
as antonyms

but if love is bound to be so complicated
with these blazes and smolderings
like blood and pain
(and blood is not like periods
but some new feeling of mine)
(and pain is yours)
if love is made up
of two different feelings
then soon love will also be called crisis

I have a crisis for you, darling
let's get married
it'll be easier for us both

we've got a crisis
we'd better split up ✖

*Translated by **Svetlana Lavochkina***

nowhere is left undamaged and where there is constant shelling. Then I arrived in a genuine paradise with palm trees, where it was summer, with pools, and where everyone was friendly, supportive and sympathetic, embracing me.

The Grammy producers sent yellow and blue flowers with a note for me to my room. Everyone was so sweet. I felt very out of place, because I came with just one set of footwear – leather boots with laces – and it was 27 degrees in Las Vegas. At the same time, I felt very much at home, primarily due to the attitude to me as an equal. This was thanks to conversations about Ukrainians as people who defend freedom and democracy around the world. I was impressed and it warmed me up somewhat emotionally.

IOC We've read you talking about how war changes language. Can you expand on this?

LY Oh, that's a very long story. However, I will try to illustrate it through examples. Look at the word "light". Light is that which makes the darkened and invisible things visible. It brings us day in the night and warms us. However, circumstances change during the war. The light switched on at night in your city during military hostilities is a threat, because the most illuminated areas are the target of enemy troops. That is why it is necessary to mask light, and the authorities and the media remind us to do so. Now, therefore, the light is no longer the light it used to be, but something which bears a threat to life.

Or there is the word "corridor", a transitional part of your home, just something that leads from the street into the house. However, during shelling people have to hide either in a bomb shelter or in a room with two load-bearing walls and no windows. That is in a corridor. My son slept in the corridor, because there isn't a place for everyone, and it's 20 minutes' walk to the nearest bomb shelter and takes forever to get through the checkpoints. So now the corridor, for every Ukrainian who was under fire, means a safe place to sleep.

There are, in addition, many new words related to modern weapons and obscene language ceases to be taboo. Even children in bomb shelters quote a famous phrase about a Russian warship [the one that was sunk in April and has been renamed in Ukraine 'Go Fuck Yourself' warship], and adults don't prohibit them from swearing.

Now imagine that you want to say something using these words that have changed their meaning. You say it, but it turns out not as you intended. And now imagine that there are already hundreds, tens of hundreds of such words. How to speak in a war-torn language? How to write in such a language? We have to invent new ways of expression. ✖

*Translated by **Stephen Komarnyckyj***

51(02):84/87|DOI:10.1177/03064220221110792

A Cassandra worth heeding

Anna Politkovskaya warned the world about Putin. As **DOMINIC CAVENDISH** introduces
an extract of her work, he explains why her words should be given a stage

'M A THEATRE critic, not a political commentator. But I'm a critic partly because I believe that the theatre can offer vital political commentary.

Surveying the output on our major stages, one question that has puzzled and alarmed me for years is: where is Anna Politkovskaya's influence? With the invasion of Ukraine, her protracted absence feels particularly shaming, and retrospectively concerning.

Politkovskaya worked tirelessly to present a damning dossier of evidence about the entrenched criminality and barbarity of Russian president Vladimir Putin's regime. The journalist spoke with countless people whose lives had been ruined by the actions of a man she dared dismiss as "a typical lieutenant colonel in the Soviet KGB" and she made statements loaded with warning about what lay ahead.

In 2002, she won the Index on Censorship Freedom of Expression Award for most courageous defence of free expression.

In her book Putin's Russia (2004), she explicitly declared: "Putin has, by chance, got his hands on enormous power and has used it to catastrophic effect … He believes he can do anything he likes with us, play with us as he sees fit, destroy us as he sees fit … In Russia we have had leaders with this outlook before. It led to tragedy, to bloodshed on a huge scale."

ABOVE: Anna Politkovskaya attends the 2005 Hay Festival in Wales, the year before she was assassinated

She gathered testimonies, at considerable risk, and was gunned down outside her Moscow flat in 2006 – a case that has never been adequately resolved.

Her murder caused an international outcry and cemented her reputation as a courageous chronicler of the darkening post-Soviet era.

For this unassuming investigative journalist to be widely translated and much garlanded gave her rare prestige while she was alive and, in theory, a posthumous capacity to shape the debate.

It might seem odd to liken her to the Greek mythological figure Cassandra – the priestess blessed with the gift of prophecy, doomed never to be believed – but in the UK at least, where heeding and acting on those warnings might just have prompted a decisive, robust response from the West, it's as if she invited chit-chat rather than a concerted call to arms.

But her harrowing, unflinching descriptions about the conduct, or rather savage misconduct, of Russian forces during the Second Chechen War and its aftermath – the apocalyptic razing of Grozny, the gross, even genocidal, violations of human rights – are the blueprint for what has taken place in Mariupol, and what was presumably intended to be replicated right across Ukraine: the subjugation and ruination

We're not remotely out of the woods yet.
And few explained how we got into them
better than she did

of an entire population. But she wasn't given the cultural weight needed to swing mass opinion here.

She talked of her stigmatisation in Russia as "the madwoman of Moscow", where the empathy she showed others, and her arguably feminine gravitation towards the least powerful victims of oppression, was held as some sign of a psychological weakness. Did we unwittingly allow a similarly sexist censorship to downgrade her personalised vignettes as "colour pieces"?

Much of her writing is so vivid it would have made a swift and potent transition to the stage. A decade ago, I pulled together a script of excerpts with a view to finding a theatrical platform for them. I put that project aside in the

Politkovskaya's journeys to hell and back need due acknowledgement, and articulation, even now – especially now

naive belief that big institutions would have registered the possibilities, and necessity, of mounting something.

Hindsight is an easy thing, but Politkovskaya's journeys to hell and back need due acknowledgement, and articulation, even now – especially now.

In an ideal world, just as there's a spirit to rename UK streets after Ukraine's president Volodymyr Zelensky, so London's Moscow Road looks like the perfect candidate for

Politkovskaya-isation.

But let's hear it, literally, for her writing. It would be better late than never for her work to be aired somehow, verbatim or not, in theatres. As far as Putin and Russia are concerned, we're not remotely out of the woods yet.

And few explained how we got into them better than she did. ✖

Dominic Cavendish is a theatre critic for The Daily Telegraph

It's Nice to Be Deaf

September 1999.
We are lying on withered autumn grass.

To be more precise, we want to lie on it, but for most of us all that's left is the dusty Chechen ground.

There are too many of us - hundreds, and there are not enough amenities for everyone.

We are the people caught in the bombing.

We didn't do anything wrong; we were just walking toward Ingushetia along the former highway, which is now all torn up by armoured vehicles.

Grozny is behind us.

We run as a herd from the war and its battles.

When the time comes, and you have to hit the ground face down, assuming a foetal position, trying to hide your head, knees and even elbows under your body - then a kind of false, sticky loneliness sneaks up on you, and you start to think, 'Why are you crouching? What are you trying to save? This life of yours that no one but you cares about?'

Why is it false?

Because you know perfectly well that this isn't really true; you have a family, and they are waiting and praying for you.

And it's sticky because of the sweat.

When you're clinging to life, you sweat a lot.

Some people are lucky, though.

When they feel that death is near, all that happens is that the hair rises on their heads.

Still, there is loneliness.

Death is the one situation where you can never find companionship.

When the diving helicopters hover over your bent back, the ground starts to resemble a death bed.

Here are the helicopters, going for another round.

They fly so low that you can see the gunners' hands and faces.

Some say that they can even see their eyes.

But this is fear talking.

The main thing is their legs, dangling carelessly in the open hatches.

As if they didn't come to kill, but to let their tired feet get some fresh air.

Their feet are big and scary, and the soles   →

→ almost seem to touch our faces.

The barrels of their guns are squeezed between their thighs.

We're frightened, but we all want to see our killers.

They seem to be laughing at us crawling comically down below - heavy old women, young girls, and children.

We can even hear their laughter.

But no, this is just another illusion; it's too noisy to hear that.

Automatic weapon fire whistles in the air around us, and someone always starts to wail along.

Has anyone been killed?

Wounded?

'Don't move. Don't raise your head. That's my advice,' a man next to me says.

He dropped to the ground right where he was, in his black suit with a white shirt and black tie.

My neighbour Vakha starts talking non-stop.

This is a good thing; it's better to talk now than to be silent.

Vahka is a land surveyor from Achkhoi-Martan, a big village not far from Ingushetia.

In wartime Chechnya, everyone is afraid of everything.

This morning, Vakha left his house wearing his suit and carrying his folder as usual, so as not to attract attention, as if he were going to work.

In fact, he had decided to flee.

'Every time,' Vakha mumbles, because you can't help mumbling with your mouth pressed to the ground, 'every time the helicopters come, I take my folder, get out some paper, and pretend to write. I think it helps.'

People nearby start to laugh quietly.

'How can paper help? What are you talking about?' a tiny, skinny man to his left mutters in a loud whisper, spitting out dirt.

'The pilots see that I'm working, that I'm not a terrorist,' the land surveyor retorts.

'And what if they think just the opposite? That you're taking down their license plate numbers?' a female body in front pipes up, gingerly shifting a bit. 'I'm all numb. When will this all end?'

'If they think that, then you're done for.'

We can't see who says this.

He is behind us.

And it's a good thing: his words are tough, sharp and pitiless, like an axe.

'There you go again. Enough of that.'

An old man's voice cuts the tough guy short.

Then he asks Vakha, 'Show me your folder, please. I'll tell the others.'

The bodies, who have been silenced by the tough guy, are eager to clutch at straws again, to enjoy an unexpected gift of momentary happiness, the last for some.

'Go ahead, show us...'

'We'll all get these folders..'

'The Russians will run out of them...'

'Putin will wonder, why are all the Chechens running around with folders duing the war? They should be carrying automatic weapons...'

'And he'll give out folders to the Feds too. All of Chechnya will be carrying folders...'

'Vahka, what colour should the folders be?'

The helicopters don't stop circling around.

The children's crying shakes the ground that is studded with people, machine guns are shooting - why don't they shut up for just a moment? - and the explosions of falling mines croak the whole time, introducing a banal note into our stay on the death bed.

That's all we need!

Still, people joke around.

Vakha defends himself meekly.

'It's all in Allah's hands,' he says.

'But say what you want, I've never been wounded with this folder. Not in the first war, and not in this one. It's always helped me.'

'So you had the folder in the first war too?' someone bursts out laughing, in a kind of nervous spasm.

'Then why are you lying on the ground, man? Why don't you get up?'

Vakha is tired of that.

'Everyone's lying on the ground. Why should I

ABOVE: A woman stands amongst the rubble of a bombed building in Grozny, Chechnya, in the early 2000s. At this time, Russian control was being re-established in the region.

be the one to get up? Why should I make myself into a target?'

'But you have your folder.'

It's the old man who cut off the tough guy, who, by the way, has been silent ever since.

The old man laughs somewhere behind us, if you can call body movements and raspy sighs against the ground laughter.

'You don't know how lucky you are, man; they might think you're counting us. And that means you're on their side.'

Vahka is silent now; it's not time for jokes. Everything in its place.

He starts blowing dust from his dirty black sleeves, breathing from somewhere under his body.

After all, this is the only thing he can do in the foetal position we've been forced to assume.

In twenty-four hours, Vakha and his magic folder will be destroyed, blown up by a mine about a mile from where we are now lying.

He'll take just a few steps away from the road into an untidy, unharvested field from that first wartime autumn.

There were already too many mines to count, and everyone to a man, including soldiers and militants, was wandering around Chechnya without a map of the minefields.

It's like playing Russian roulette.

Vahka walks to that side not because he has to, but simply because he's exhausted from waiting.

The line to the passport check-point was too long.

It consisted mostly of us jokers, the new family he'd prepared to die with the day before, lying →

→ on a different field.

Now dead, Vahka lies on a field again, but this time fearlessly, with his wounded face looking up and his hands spread wider than they've ever been in his life.

The left hand is about ten yards from his black jacket, which has been torn to pieces.

The right hand is a bit closer, about five steps away.

And Vakha's legs are quite a problem: they disappear, most likely turning into dust at the time of the explosion and flying away with the wind.

His folder with its blank sheets of paper meets the same fate.

It saved him from the helicopters, but it can't save him from the mines.

Then two soldiers carefully approach Vakha from the checkpoint with the long line. One of them is young and scrawny; he looks like he's fifteen years old, and his helmet and boots are too big.

The second is a bit older and bigger, well-built, with his hands in the pockets of his camouflage pants.

The first starts crying softly, dirtying his face as he wipes his tears, and turns around, not having the heart to look.

The second smacks him on the back of the head, and the first soldiers shuts up immediately, like an alarm clock that's been turned off with a slap of the hand so that a person can continue sleeping in the morning.

The Chechens in line buy an 'emergency reserve' big black plastic sack for 'Cargo 200' from these soldiers' lieutenant.

Then they gather Vakha's remains and spend quite a while discussing where to bring them.

To his mother, wife, and children in the camp at Ingushetia?

Or to his empty house in Achkhoi-Martan?

Reason prevails - the body should be brought to Achkhoi, of course.

It will be buried there anyway, in the family cemetery. So why waste money lugging it to Ingushetia?

You need to bribe a lot of people to get there.

At the Kavkaz checkpoint, the border between this war and the rest of the world, you need to pay twice, once each way.

And you'd have to pay two or three times as much for a corpse, depending on the commander's mood that day.

.... But for now, Vakha will be alive and well for 24 hours.

And we continue to lie on the field on the outskirts of Gekhi, hoping to get away from the helicopters, and almost believing in a happy future.

After all, it's only the beginning of the war, the first days of October 1999.

It seems to us that the fighting won't last too long, and that the refugees will soon be able to return to their homes.

All we have to do is survive this day, and things will straighten themselves out.

At one point, Vakha becomes bolder - after all, when there is danger for too long, everything gets to be dull and boring.

Ignoring the helicopters, he suddenly turns over onto his side.

And in a normal human way, without earth in his mouth, he begins to talk about his family - his six children, who had left Achkoi a week ago for Ingushetia along with his mother, wife, and two unmarried sisters.

They're the ones he's trying to make his way to.

Off to the side, Gekhi is being bombed.

Probably as fiercely and continuously as Konigsberg was in World War II.

Vakha turns face down again.

'There were so many refugees from Grozny gathered there - a real nightmare,' he says, distracted from the topic of his family and engrossed in the rhythm of the attackers' mounting, irrational bombing of their own people.

'Thousands, probably. In the last bombing, a week ago, a hospital was destroyed, and the sick and wounded were taken away. Where will they take the wounded now?'

The women are quietly wailing, and shushing the children so they don't wail, as if the children weren't people too.

The splashing sounds emitted by the weapons swarm around us from all sides, not letting our minds rest.

Although it's been only about half an hour since the beginning of the helicopter attack, it seems like half a day, enough time to recall most of your life.
People gradually start to lose their self-control.
Cries of desperation can be heard; men are sobbing.

But not all of them.
Among us are some thirteen - or fourteen-year-olds.
They are excitedly and joyfully discussing which weapon is being used at a given moment.
And what else can they do besides demonstrate their thorough knowledge?
They've been learning modern weapon terminology their whole conscious lives, since the Chechen war began, for nearly ten years.

Between the teenagers and us, a little boy is quietly crawling around. He is probably six years old, thin and sad-looking.
He isn't screaming, crying, or grabbing his mother, but looking around thoughtfully and saying, 'It's nice to be deaf' in a simple, calm, even everyday voice.
As if he were saying 'It's nice to play ball'.

Right then the 'hail' overtakes us.
There is no greater torture for a person's hearing, not to mention life, in war.
The hail comes from the late twentieth-century version of the Katyusha rocket launcher.
It whistles and hisses for a long time.
But if you can already hear it, that means it's past you, and death, though it was nearby, has chosen someone else for the time being.
And you laugh about this.

The hail turns you into an inhuman beast that has learned to rejooice in someone else's misfortune.
The boy, who is lying comfortably on a grass bush pillow despite the circumstances, sums it up this way:
'The deaf can't hear any of this. And so they're not afraid.'

Vakha quietly pulls the boy closer, hugs him, and gives him some candy from the pocket of his black jacket.

'What's your name?' Vakha asks, crying softly.
'Sharpuddin,' the boy answers, surprised to see a grown man crying.
'It would be even better, Sharpuddin, if we could become blind, mute and stupid.' Vakha's eyes dry up under the boy's gaze.
'But we're not. And yet we have to survive anyway.'

The helicopters fly away after about five minutes, and the hail falls silent.
The raid is over.
People begin to pick themselves up at once and shake themselves off.
Someone praises Allah.
The field becomes lively.
The women run to look for trucks for the wounded, and the men carry the dead to one place.
A day and night pass.
The boy, Sharpuddin, goes up to the men who are collecting Vahka's remains in a black bag, and silently begins to help them.
They sternly shoo him away like a dog, for his own good, but his mother objects.
She says that her son was the last child that Vakha caressed in his life.
And then Sharpuddin is allowed to help. ✖

From **Anna Politkovskaya**'s A Small Corner of Hell: Dispatches from Chechnya (The University of Chicago Press), translated by **Alexander Burry** and **Tatiana Tulchinsky**

51(02):88/93|DOI:10.1177/03064220221110793

Poetic injustice

Writers in Ukraine are at risk once again. **STEPHEN KOMARNYCKYJ** explores how an anthology of literature gives an insight into past and present

RIGHT: Portrait of Ukrainian poet Maik Yohansen, who in 1934 joined the Soviet Writer's Union of Ukraine

UKRAINE HAS A history of silenced writers, with a legacy that sheds light on the current war. In The Executed Renaissance, a 1959 anthology published in Paris by Ukrainian literary critic Yurii Lavrinenko, their voices live on. The 20th century saw a generation of Ukrainian authors destroyed by Joseph Stalin, but through this anthology some of the country's most prominent work has been salvaged.

There is a complex story of censorship behind this collection. Ukrainian literature was subject to severe legal restrictions under the Tsars, with one minister of the interior notoriously saying: "There is no Ukrainian language." After the Russian empire fell, Ukraine was briefly independent – from 1917 until 1921 – before being incorporated into the Soviet Union following its conquest by the Bolsheviks.

During the 1920s, the Soviets sought to embed their regime in the republics they had created across the ruined empire, by using their native languages. Ukraine, however, was different. Russians had always struggled with the idea that Ukraine was not part of Russia.

After the fall of the empire, Ukrainians embraced the opportunity to write in a language that had for so long been largely forbidden. Their writing was naturally radical, because to write in Ukrainian was, by definition, to oppose imperial orthodoxy and colonisation.

Under imperial Russian rule, most Ukrainians had been serfs, including their brilliant national poet Taras Shevchenko. His poems, such as

Caucasus, attacked the subjugation of people under Russian rule.

Another Ukrainian poet, Lesya Ukrainka, was a radical feminist whose plays featured strong female heroines and patriarchy.

The writers of the 1920s embraced futurism and symbolism, and – while notionally loyal to communist ideology – a dangerous new autonomy was in the air. The Bolsheviks were as imperialist as their Tsarist predecessors. From 1929 onwards, the machinery of mass executions, deportations, gulags and a genocidal forced famine known as the Holodomor, were unleashed on Ukraine. The mass executions would ultimately merge with the Soviet-wide Great Terror, but their Ukrainian dimension is crucial to understanding both Soviet history and Russia's current assault on Ukraine.

Lavrinenko barely survived the destruction himself, but managed to escape the Soviet Union in World War II. He pieced together as much work of silenced Ukrainian authors as he could, using material published between 1917 and 1933, which was subsequently censored. The Executed Renaissance was born.

Maik Yohansen, one of the poets Lavrinenko anthologised, celebrates the small, fleeting moments of life, such as the piece published here, where a voice calls through the fog. The second poem is both a bizarre moment of imagination and a call for a genuine global revolution, completely alien to the regime that would ultimately murder him.

Lavrinenko's anthology could not capture all the authors the Soviets

destroyed. One notable writer, the poet Lidiya Mohylianska, also known as Lada, was not included. She was born in Chernihiv and arrested in 1929 for criticising collectivisation, and executed by firing squad in 1937. The first of her poems published here is a beautiful meditation on the passing of summer into autumn, ahead of its time technically.

However, the second poem is extraordinarily modern, a foreshadowing of Ted Hughes's Crow in terms of metaphor and freedom of form. It is an anguished appeal for compassion that speaks to the events in Ukraine today.

According to one estimate, of the 259 writers active in Ukraine at the beginning of the 1930s, only 36 were still writing by the end of the decade. The Soviets subsequently rekindled Ukrainian patriotism in World War II to motivate the 4.5 million Ukrainian soldiers in the Red Army, but then crushed the literary revival which followed in the 1960s.

However, glasnost – an attempt to galvanise the economy via political liberalisation while retaining control – would ultimately reignite Ukrainian nationhood.

Further attempts to suppress it culminated in the current war. Russia is destroying Ukrainian books in occupied areas, and Ukrainian author Volodymyr Vakulenko and his son were abducted from Izium by Russian forces in March.

When we look at the authors of The Executed Renaissance now, we can see they are not simply a lesson from the past. They are part of a historical process we are watching unfold in the massacres perpetrated across central and eastern Ukraine. ✖

Stephen Komarnyckyj is an award-winning British-Ukrainian poet, journalist and translator

Poems by MAIK YOHANSEN

Return!

The voice came from the fog
            Like a bird
My heart leapt, my hands lowered into the past,
A tram broke the silence then tore into view.
I heard how the day burned, how the grass grew,
Hey, higher than the groves and skylarks so
            That the birds angrily
    tore and pecked it.
                        And again
                        Return!
Lower
            And less audible than the distant murmur
                                    Of the capital,
The word died in its countless pavements.

Poetry

We have birthed so many words me and you,
That you could populate the moon with them
Dreamed out so many dreams so blue
That our children frolic on all the planets.

We have sailed all round the sea you and me
And the Pacific, all of its bays
The moon peered from clouds a jackal's eye
Above our heads Lianas dreamed.

We worked in the rice field too and were beaten
By white people and all the wounds
Of the world were on your hands and all
Its pain and anger in my broad breast.

So we will build the last barricades
And you will shoot the very last king
And on the Earth great councils will come,
And you will die, my darling.

RIGHT: A woman visits a book market stand in Odessa,
Ukraine. Ukrainian writers have a long history of being
silenced in the country

Poems by LADA MOHYLIANSKA

Here is Autumn... cheerful horse clop...
The garden dreams its dog rose, only
Yesterday we unlocked summer's treasury
With a gold key.

Only yesterday the lightning cockily
Fine as a spider web in the sky...
Today the wind has scattered bundles
Of yellow leaves on the canal.

When they died they saw the eyes of rifles
Like the dead eyeholes of skulls...
And then laid... face up in the grass...
And the wind plucked the strings of the cold night.

When they died they passed, unnoticed and quietly,
Their pale lips whispered innocent prayers.
The morning sun shone on a mound of earth
And the guard's dark shadow that was their cross.

Cornflowers laughed nearby, at the boundary
And morning bustled with its wild festivity...
He is crucified! Do you see! Hear! Come! Help!
Crucified! ✖

Translated by Stephen Komarnyckyj

51(02):94/95|DOI:10.1177/03064220221110794

Banking on Russia's poetic spirit

One of the translators behind a new project to get anti-war Russian poetry out, **MARIA BLOSHTEYN**, introduces it and one of its poets

"MANY RUSSIANS HAVE voiced concerns that this war may have rendered a fatal blow to Russian culture as an idea," said poet and translator Yulia Fridman. A mother of four, she is a physicist by training, works as a research scientist and was recently fined for taking part in a demonstration protesting the war in Ukraine. Born in Novosibirsk, Siberia, in 1970, she had long been based in Moscow but is currently out of the country.

Fridman's poems are closely connected to Russian counterculture and, like the one featured below and published exclusively for Index, prove

that dissent still exists in the country – you just have to know where to look.

In this case it's the Kopilka Project. I discovered Fridman's poem, with its apocalyptic yet unnervingly plausible vision of the Kremlin's war against Ukraine – and then against the entire world – in the Kopilka Project. It's a new, extraordinary repository of anti-war poetry by Russian speakers from around the world, today numbering more than 600 pages, with more than 100 poets involved, and growing.

It was founded by poets and translators based in the USA – Julia Nemirovskaya, Dmitry Manin, Anya

Krushelnitskaya, Irina Mashinsky and Andrei Burago – and its aim is to collect Russophone poems that speak out against the war in Ukraine and to make them accessible to translators and publishers worldwide. "Kopilka" translates from Russian as "piggy bank" and, speaking to Index, Nemirovskaya said they consider their "effort as throwing a tiny copper coin into a bigger Kopilka, the collective effort to defeat Putin." In many ways it's as close to the Cold War idea of *samizdat* - the clandestine distribution of works banned by the state - as you get today.

"We began to collect wartime poetry at the onset of Putin's war. Since our small volunteer group is based in the US and cannot be persecuted by the Russian government, we collected anti-war works of the poets who lived in Russia. It was a way to keep those poems safe," said Nemirovskaya, adding:

"The mere fact that so many anti-war poems are being written by so many good poets is a strong statement on the war's impact on artistic expression. I remember in his lecture on Vladimir Vernardsky, V. V. Ivanov said that large-scale tragedies created voids in *"noosfera"*; the voids were then filled by works of poets, artists, musicians and philosophers. This explanation is probably a bit simplistic. Still, there is some universal order that provides for a more intense intellectual activity during wars and revolutions. Our Kopilka is a testimony to that."

Nemirovskaya describes poetry as "a soldier fighting for the right cause".

When I asked Fridman to comment on what it's like to be part of this cause and to be writing poems in Russian within the Russian cultural space during the war against Ukraine, she said she'd "rather see those poets who do not consider themselves Russian poets any more alive and well, reunited with their loved ones, living in a free country taken back from the occupiers. If anything can benefit Russian culture at this point, I feel it's that one thing".

She also spoke of the Russian poets who live in Ukraine and its changing, difficult landscape. One has serious health problems.

"When the sirens sound, he cannot go down to the shelter himself and is always trying to make his mother, daughter and cat go to the shelter without him … he occasionally succeeds. There was a time when, judging by his occasional remarks, I used to think of him as pro-Russian, but that was before the war began. Now he calls himself a Martian poet," she said.

Fridman, who questions the future of the Russian language, speaks of another poet, also in Ukraine, who has not written in Russian since 2014.

"That year he was forced to leave his home to the new regime and settle in the town of Sumy, in north-eastern Ukraine with his family. On February 24 of this year everything changed. He helped his wife and kids get safely to Poland, gave whatever food he had in storage to his neighbours and joined the Ukrainian military forces. Sometimes I hear from him – he sounds almost happy and hates everything Russian. He is a Ukrainian poet." ✖

Maria Bloshteyn is a Russian translator and a scholar of comparative literature and cultural studies

*Additional research by **Jemimah Steinfeld***

When we had liberated Ukraine from the Nazis

Yulia Fridman

When we had liberated Ukraine from the Nazis,
Poland from Martians, Finland from dog-headed men,
the Earth sprouted fragrant cocaine-smelling blossoms,
and our tankmen got high on their magical scent.

Lithuania became a hotbed for galactic snails
from Epsilon of Andromeda, that cold crimson star;
they hid among salad greens and other plants,
we bombed it flat – no choice but go that far.

We were compelled to raze Estonia from the map,
since the ichthyosaurs took over step by step,
they arrived from Alfa Centaurus, on an orbital lap,
all of them devotees of Astarte's gory sect.

In Latvia too, we destroyed all signs of life,
we had no choice – the West forced our hand!
It propagated noxious microbes there,
as the crypto-science gurus let us understand.

Now all nations are free, they write us from Eden,
and all sundry creatures, both furred and feathered –
and Moscow extends from horizon to distant horizon,
from sandstorm to sandstorm in the new global desert. ✖

*Translated by **Maria Bloshteyn***

51(02):96/97|DOI:10.1177/03064220221110795

Metaphors and madness

The writer **EDUARDO HALFON** speaks to **JEMIMAH STEINFELD** on outsmarting censors and how the dangers of living in Guatemala are forcing his friends to adopt extreme routines. Plus a new, exclusive short story

"GUATEMALA'S GREATEST WRITERS are all buried outside Guatemala. You have generations of writers and poets and dramatists and journalists either disappearing – being killed off – or fleeing." These were the words of Guatemalan author Eduardo Halfon, a winner of the country's National Prize in Literature with almost 20 books to his name, including Mourning, which won the Edward Lewis Wallant Award and the International Latino Book Award.

Halfon is yet another Guatemalan writer working from outside the country of his birth. He was speaking with Index in a video call from his current home in Berlin. Halfon says he has been spared the extremes of censorship as a result of writing fiction, which provides him a degree of protection. "What I say is coded. It's hidden within a metaphor or it's someone else's voice saying it." Add to this a low readership of fiction in the country (according to Halfon "nobody reads novels") and the novelist has a degree of creative freedom.

"It's ironic, isn't it, that fiction allows me to say the truth?" he said.

And yet for all that, Halfon has still been at the receiving end of serious threats. After publishing his first novel in 2003, he met a friend at a bar who told him to leave the country as soon as possible; later he was visited at home by someone he barely knew brandishing a gun and giving him a warning.

"That's the way you get threatened in Guatemala. It's never a direct threat [from those in power]. You're never going to get directly threatened or explain why you are being threatened. It's a way of provoking a general fear. And this has been going on for decades. All of these military dictatorships were just based on fear and silencing people."

Halfon believes that his run-ins are the result of interviews he has done, and so he tries to avoid doing them in Guatemala itself.

He hasn't let the gun experience deter him. While he writes mainly in Spanish, his fourth English novel (Canción) is due out in September.

ABOVE: Guatemalan author Eduardo Halfon

He's in no rush to return to Guatemala. The "culture of fear", as he terms it, is worse today than before.

"The climate there is as dangerous as I've ever seen it," he said, explaining how journalists are currently fleeing on a weekly basis, as are judges.

"If you're not a corrupt judge and you're trying to do right you have to either leave or you're killed."

In order to survive in the country, Halfon says Guatemalans have normalised behaviours that elsewhere would be considered extreme. "The psychotic manifestations of living in that danger", as Halfon terms it, is perhaps best exemplified by the story of his friend, who drives with and speaks to a mannequin in the passenger seat at all times in an effort not to be targeted in her car. "And this friend of mine considers it absolutely normal that she would have to live this way," he added.

Guatemalans have also developed an indirect way of talking, avoiding certain words entirely. "Genocide" is one, despite the massacre, forced disappearance and torture of the country's indigenous Maya people by the security forces on and off for decades.

"They won't even say it. It's a dirty word. There's a percentage of the population – which is a small percentage but a powerful percentage – who deny that genocide took place, so they want to just silence the word. The last time I said it in an interview one of my father's friends (who is Jewish and a lawyer) called my father and asked me to stop saying it. He said no genocide had ever taken place."

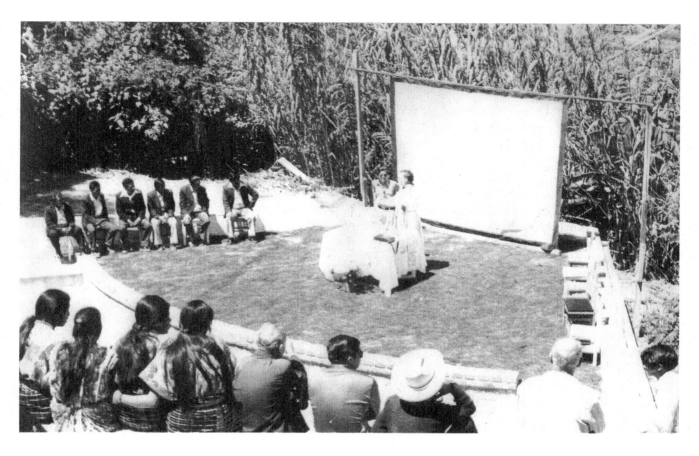

OPPOSITE & ABOVE: The only remaining images of the amphitheatre, where for a short while locals enjoyed films on a variety of topics

Then there's "land reform". "It's another one of those words that is dangerous to utter in Guatemala because the oligarchs, the rich, the land-owners feel threatened."

Halfon unites these taboo words in the short story overleaf, published for the first time here. It tells the story of doctors who built and ran an amphitheatre in the 1970s to air a mixture of entertaining and educational films for the indigenous people of the area. Some films were even shot by the locals, who were taught how to

operate cameras as part of the project. The story is based on a true story, with some fictional embellishments. Halfon, who knows the doctor personally, reflects on the film project with awe – putting a camera into people's hands and using stories to "try and reach those who needed reaching" was "a heroic effort". The authorities took a different approach. The makeshift cinema was quickly shut down and all footage, bar the two images pictured here, were lost.

"The military government could not allow a place for the indigenous people to learn, to heal," he noted.

In the story, which follows the doctor and another man walking through

terrain where the amphitheatre was, a discussion ensues on *zombobos* – huge ants that would descend on the area during the wet season.

"I haven't seen one in years and as a kid they were everywhere."

Halfon first left Guatemala at the age of 10. He has memories of making the ants fight [two together in a box] and of the indigenous people eating them at special occasions. Now, due to climate change and the excessive use of agri-chemicals, they're gone.

"What those *zombobos* represent is not just the death of a vital animal but also of a culture," he said.

It all fits into the pattern of Guatemalan history, which Halfon describes as "a history of silence". The only positive is that the country still has individuals like Halfon willing to speak, even if from afar. ✖

 This friend of mine considers it absolutely normal that she would have to live this way

Jemimah Steinfeld is editor-in-chief of Index ➔

The Amphitheatre

For Juan José Hurtado, in memoriam

HE HANDED ME a torch of burning ocote. Hold it up like this, he said, showing me how with his own. Then I received from him an ancient clay *tinaja*. I liked the feel of the cold damp earth in my hand, as if I were holding a piece of the past, of a time more diaphanous and primitive and painted in shades of ochre. Let's see if we get lucky and one of them falls, he said. We began to walk slowly through the now empty and dark streets of San Juan Sacatepéquez.

I thought I felt a soft drizzle on my face. Although it could have also been nothing more than the evening mist. Or my nerves. We passed the vacant lot where I had left my car. We passed some market stalls around the central plaza, already closed and covered with black and blue plastic tarps. We passed a cantina that was probably a brothel. We passed a bundle of green bananas lying in the middle of the street. We passed a row of crumbling houses, and I remembered the earthquake of 1976. We passed a small bridge that crossed a black and rancid creek. We passed by a large piece of land full of apple trees and something that in the night looked to me like a grandstand descending to a small stage. Like an amphitheatre in ruins — like the bleachers of an amphitheatre in ruins. I asked Ramón what it was and he stopped and told me it had been a movie theatre. But years ago, he said. When I was young.

He placed his clay *tinaja* on the ground, pressed between his black rubber boots. He took a cigarette out of the pack of menthol Rubios and lit it with the fire of his torch. I accepted one. I also lit it with the fire of my torch. I felt prehistoric.

Ramón told me that, in the seventies, some doctors from the city came to the village on weekends and showed there, pointing to the small amphitheatre with his cigarette, all kinds of movies. He told me that the doctors had built it themselves, among the apple trees. He told me that as a young man he had seen there movies of Cantinflas and of Pedro Infante and some cowboy movies. He told me that the doctors also showed short films, in Kaqchikel, made by the villagers themselves. He told me that the doctors had a small sixteen-millimeter camera and they would give it to the local people and teach them how to use it and ask them to make very short films in Kaqchikel about nature, about basic health, about life in the village. He told me that the doctors would then show those short films in the middle of the Cantinflas and Pedro Infante and cowboy movies.

I looked down at the amphitheatre among the apple trees (I smelled or thought I smelled the apple trees in the night). I noticed that the bleachers were overgrown, abandoned, useless, and I suddenly imagined all the indigenous people of San Juan Sacatepéquez sitting there as they watched the short, blurry, sixteen-millimetre films in Kaqchikel, made by themselves. I asked Ramón what had happened to the movie theatre. Oh, he said, it ceased to exist. And his voice hurried to hide in the night. But it wasn't difficult for me to guess the rest of the story, to guess why something like that could not exist (to use his word) in the Guatemala of the seventies. I asked Ramón what the short films had been like, if he remembered any of them. But he just threw away his cigarette, crushed it into the ground with his black rubber boot, and kept walking.

*

Soon, almost without realising it, we had left the outskirts of the village. We kept moving forward and reached a trail and began to walk among old oak trees, up the mountain. The ground was →

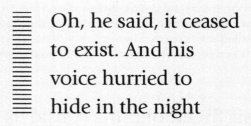

Oh, he said, it ceased to exist. And his voice hurried to hide in the night

→ muddy and slippery. I looked back fleetingly. The entire village had disappeared.

In front of me, while hacking away some loose branches from the trail with his machete, Ramón was telling me about the origin of the village's name. San Juan, he said, is for John the Baptist, the patron saint of the municipality. Sacatepéquez, he said, is actually two words in Kaqchikel. *Sacat*, which means grass. And *tepec*, which means hill. I asked him about the origin and meaning of his own name. Ramón López Chumil, he announced softly but not without pride. Ramón López is for my father Ramón López and my grandfather Ramón López and my great-grandfather Ramón López. Chumil, he said, is my mother's last name. It means star, in Kaqchikel.

After a while we stopped to rest and I asked Ramón in a whisper (as if my voice might scare them away) if he had seen any already. Not one, he said. They haven't come out. Not as many come out as before, he said and spat a long slimy drool to the ground. He was silent for a moment, panting lightly, as he tucked the hem of his pants into the big black rubber boots.

Before, when I was a boy, he said, as soon as the first rains came in May, we would go up the mountain with my father and catch *zompopos de mayo*. They would fall from the sky, he said with the momentousness of a preacher. Imagine that. They would just fall from the sky and fly towards the flames of the ocote and with my father we would pick them up from the ground and put them in our *tinajas*. There wasn't enough room for so many in our *tinajas*. Then we would return to the house and my mother would throw them all into a basin full of water, to wash them before removing their wings and legs and heads, since one only eats the small round body of a *zompopo*. She would then put the round bodies on the comal and toast them with a pinch of salt. I thought I saw Ramón smile in the amber light. Very tasty, he said. Only for special occasions.

We continued through the forest in silence, me slipping a little in the mud with each step, waiting for the *zompopos* to fall from the sky and fly into

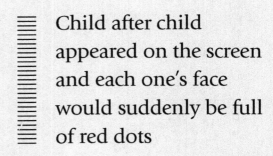

Child after child appeared on the screen and each one's face would suddenly be full of red dots

the flames of my torch. I wanted to see them, to catch them, to savour for the first time that tasty and salty and crunchy snack reserved only for special occasions.

We reached the top of the mountain. Ramon, crouching, his gaze sleepy or resigned, was silent. I thought about telling him not to worry, that I understood that the sky had already been emptied of *zompopos* (I would have to wait a few years before finally tasting one, on a not very special occasion, inside a nameless dining room on the shore of Lake Amatitlán). But I just asked him for another cigarette. And we both waited hopelessly as we smoked in the minty muffle of the night, our torches by now barely lit, our ancient clay *tinajas* almost forgotten on the ground.

*

There was a short film about a vaccine, Ramón suddenly said in the half-light. Among the films the villagers made, he added, for the doctors from the city. Although he was still crouching in front of me, I could barely see him in the moonless night. Chikop, it said on the screen at the beginning of that short film, said Ramon's voice in the darkness. Chikop, I repeated. It means little animal, in Kaqchikel, he said. First, he went on, there appeared on the screen a boy from the village, his face all painted with red dots. Then a healthy boy appeared next to him, but after a while that boy's face was also covered with red dots. Child after child appeared on the screen and each one's face would suddenly be full of red dots. Chikop, said the voice in

Kaqchikel. Not God, said the voice in Kaqchikel. Then a syringe appeared on the screen and the voice in Kaqchikel said that the red dots could be removed with a vaccine. That it was free, said the voice in Kaqchikel, that one could come there on weekends to get the vaccine from the doctors from the city. Then all the children would be on the screen together, playing happily, their faces clean. And the film ended.

＊

There was a short film about the cat technique, Ramón said. That's what the doctors from the city called it, the cat technique. I again felt a gentle drizzle on my face. The only light came from the glow of the embers of our ocotes. On the screen there was a man walking through the forest, said Ramón's voice in the night. The man then pulled down his pants and squatted right there in the forest and relieved himself next to a nearby bush. Then the man's fingers appeared on the screen throwing dirt on his droppings, covering them with dirt using his fingers. Ramón made a brief pause, necessary to smoke or maybe to overcome his modesty. And a voice in Kaqchikel said that one had to do as a cat does.

＊

There was a film of a dragonfly, Ramón said in the night. *B'atz'ibal*, said a voice on the screen. It means devil's needle, in Kaqchikel, he said. The dragonfly on the screen was crashing against the glass of a window. Over and over and over. The dragonfly wanted to go out, but the window was

The only thing that moved forward was the film. The bare feet of the villagers never moved forward

closed. A voice in Kaqchikel said that the nature of a dragonfly is to fly back to the banks of the river.

＊

There was a film of the villager's feet, Ramón said. The villagers were all lined up. They were waiting for something. But on the screen were only their bare feet. The film on the screen moved forward in the line, but one only saw the bare feet of the villagers. Nothing else. Just bare feet. Bare feet of men. Bare feet of women. Bare feet of children. Bare feet of old people. Many bare feet. All in a line, as if hoping to move forward toward something. But the only thing that moved forward was the film. The bare feet of the villagers never moved forward. *K'o ak'wala' taq winäq choj chik nimoymot yetzu'un*, said the voice in Kaqchikel. There are people who are still young and no longer see well.

＊

There was a short film about a half-naked woman, Ramón said. I could now barely make out his faint silhouette crouching and small in the night, but I was sure he had said it to me with the mischievousness of that child sitting in the amphitheatre among the apple trees, back in the seventies. I heard him exhale a puff of smoke. First a cow appeared, Ramón said, and a voice in Kaqchikel said that the mother cow's milk was for the calf. Then a goat appeared, and a voice in Kaqchikel said that the mother goat's milk was for the kid. Then a dog appeared, and a voice in Kaqchikel said that the mother dog's milk was for the puppy. Then a woman from the village appeared, he said, and she pulled out one of her big brown breasts, and a voice in Kaqchikel said that the mother's milk was for the baby. Ramón laughed softly, as if with shyness, or as if with cunning, or as if with the serenity of his years. In the night, somewhere near us, a frog chirped. ✖

Eduardo Halfon is an award-winning author

51(02):98/103|DOI:10.1177/03064220221110796

LEFT: Nikan Khosravi, the lead singer and guitarist of Confess, who was jailed for his music

Metal shows its mettle

Sent to Tehran's notorious Evin prison because of their music, the leaders of the Iranian heavy metal band Confess tell **GUILHERME OSINSKI** how their ordeal turned into inspiration

HEAVY METAL MUSIC has a bad reputation in Iran. Most commonly associated with the Devil, anti-religious sentiment and violent behaviour, it's the reason why Nikan Khosravi and Arash Ilkhani, founders of Confess, were arrested in 2015. Now living in Norway, they released their third studio album, Revenge at All Costs, earlier this year, their first since they fled Iran. They say it is "a crude story of oppression and catharsis but, above all, the determination to prevail".

They were kept in Tehran's Evin prison for 18 months charged with blasphemy after they released Thorn Within, a song raising doubts about God's existence. In jail, they awaited trial with the fear of a death sentence hanging over them; Khosravi also endured two months in solitary confinement – 23 hours a day without seeing a single person and barely sleeping as the lights were never turned off. This experience became the inspiration for their music.

"Since day one in our catalogue you'll find songs about suppression, oppression, religion, war," said Khosravi, the band's lead singer and guitarist. "As someone who was doing protest art, that was a kind of gift that was given to me. In the beginning I didn't notice, but they were putting gallons and gallons of fuel in my tank."

He said he had two options.

"I could sit in a corner, fist full of pills, be depressed and cry. Or I could just run through my fear and fight it instead of complaining that life didn't give me a chance and put me in jail. Yes, it's a government and it's a whole regime, but in the end they could not silence us. Now it's a bigger responsibility, I feel I'm obligated to talk about it."

Khosravi believes Iran has become a fascist regime which uses censorship as its ally. This affects all aspects of the country, including music.

"Heavy metal is a very hot topic in Iran. Since most of the songs are in English, they always think you are insulting God," he said, adding that anyone making metal music was labelled as satanic.

Ilkhani added: "They've been against it since day one, even when they didn't know what it was. For example [US heavy metal band] Slipknot – they see they are wearing masks and they think, 'Why are they hiding their identity?'"

That said, Ilkhani thinks heavy metal is now more known and accepted than before, and Khosravi feels Confess has had a positive impact.

"Bands like us pushed the boundaries. We brought this type of music from your headphones to your speakers in the living room. I could see the difference from when I was 12 to the time I was 19 – a bigger fan base," he said, adding that heavy metal has begun to be seen as just a different sound.

In order to avoid prison again, Ilkhani and Khosravi fled to Norway with the help of European organisations that work with persecuted artists. Three local musicians have joined Confess, and both Khosravi and Ilkhani say they feel more comfortable and free there.

"You can see religion is here, but at the same time there are a huge number of people who don't believe in God. There is this diversity that I call democracy. You can have a church [and]

a bar and you can choose whatever you want," Khosravi told Index.

Speaking of watching a metal show in an abandoned church he said: "Just imagine how big my eyes were! And it was only the first month I was there, so imagine my cultural shock."

The pair share advice for musicians going through similar situations.

"Two things: you can leave everything aside [and] go live a normal life. The other side is taking everything and turning it into revenge, so you don't leave life behind," said Ilkhani.

RIGHT: Arash Ilkhani from Iranian band Confess. Ilkhani says the government in Iran has always been against heavy metal, equating it with worship of the devil

And Khosravi added: "My biggest advice would be to never give up on your hopes and dreams. Life won't get easier, you just get stronger." ✖

Guilherme Osinski is editorial assistant at Index

51(02):104/105|DOI:10.1177/03064220221110797

Evin

Waking up in jail!
Morgue of living, buried inside the whale's
[BELLY!]
Hope to get out on bail! I'm following my tail,
Interrogator says I'll get hanged [FAIRLY!]
Elimination, Discrimination, From now on I'm all on my own!
Investigation, Interrogation, They're gonna crush my every bone!

23/7 locked up in a cell!
Solitary confinement will be my [CASKET!]
Fighting on for my beliefs...
What's the point if I sell out my dreams to buy my fucking last breath?

I saw my faith stepped on!
My youth's not gonna die when I'm dead gone!
History remembers the names son!
When sun is set, you go be the dawn!
When sun is set, you go be the dawn!

Having bad bunch as the [INMATES!]
If I get lucky, they'll give me fucking 6 years!
Showing me [PICTURES!], If I give them names,
Maybe they whisper something into judge's ears!

Time's not spending!

Dismembered memories with me, who knows for how many years?
I can't burst into tears!
This is war they can't bring me on my knees!
Court of injustice waits for me!
To get me on the long run, to be [DECEASED!]
Execution by the hands of the [JACKALS!]
Either I'll open the minds or my mind get [HACKLES UP!]

I saw my faith stepped on!
My youth's not gonna die when I'm dead gone!
History remembers the names son!
When sun is set, you go be the dawn!
When sun is set, you go be the dawn!

One's life will be taken by the name of your lord!
They can get my body, not the soul!
Taking me to heaven by force? I don't want that!
Went to hEVIN in -Hell-! That's my life man...
Walls walls walls [BROKE 'EM ALL OUT!]
Tons of bricks, one fist! [RULED 'EM OUT!]
Let it be known that religion has no ruth!
Got into pen (penitentiary) for one pen that wrote the truth!

I saw my faith stepped on!
My youth's not gonna die when I'm dead gone!
History remembers the names son!
When sun is set, you go be the dawn!
When sun is set, you go be the dawn! ✖

END NOTE

America's coming crucible

The news that the USA overturned Roe v Wade, which has protected the rights to abortion for almost 50 years, shook the country – and the world. **JO-ANN MORT** examines its impact on free expression

WOMEN IN THE USA have lost control over their bodies. They also face a void in the sharing of necessary information.

At the end of June, the US Supreme Court overturned its landmark 1973 ruling, Roe v Wade – the decision that led to abortion becoming a federal constitutional right. It said the US Constitution "does not confer a right to abortion" and "the authority to regulate abortion is returned to the people and their elected representatives". Almost immediately several states moved to outlaw abortion.

Protests erupted across the country (with some protesters being teargassed in response). Eight states immediately banned abortions. According to the Guttmacher Institute, 22 of the 50 US states have laws or constitutional amendments in place that will ban abortion now that Roe v Wade is revoked. Pro-choice legislators in states that have unused "trigger" laws on the books are frantically researching new legislation to supersede these old laws.

In the decades since abortion rights were confirmed by the Supreme Court, they had already become increasingly unequal. Where you live and, of course, how much money you have decide your access to healthcare.

As with everything, those with means will gain access and those most vulnerable will be at risk.

Along with access, and almost as important, there is a public sentiment divide in the USA that already impacts women's willingness to get an abortion. The country is "the red versus the

ABOVE: Demonstrators chant slogans through a megaphone, as pro-choice protests erupt across the USA following the Roe v Wade leak in May

blue", not "the red, white and blue".

The USA is an alignment of states that are increasingly warring against the federal patchwork. Cultural norms diverge profoundly across the land.

Surveillance of all kinds is becoming legal, including in Texas against healthcare workers and doctors, and those assisting women travelling for abortions. Underground networks to

help them are already in place and are being encouraged by activists, but they will probably have to burrow deeper underground to help women who want abortions to cross state lines and to access the abortion pill.

Phone calls and any easily traceable messaging can be subpoenaed. Just as in an authoritarian regime, the use of encrypted texting apps such as Signal are gaining ground to protect women.

Especially hard hit will be teenagers. According to the American Civil Liberties Union, almost 350,000 US teenagers under the age of 18 become pregnant each year, and the pregnancies are overwhelmingly unintended. Most involve a parent in their decision, and 31% of the pregnancies result in abortions.

As anyone complicit in providing abortion aid becomes legally at risk, any public support for abortion rights or abortion providers will be fair game for attack.

If it takes a village to raise a child, it takes a village, too, to keep a teenager safe. But how will families and their support systems within communities cope with public witch-hunts that corner women and young girls in need?

Public speech, free and unhindered, is critically important to keep women safe. New draconian laws will make it harder for women to search for the care they need, endanger women in violent relationships, and create a culture of fear that re-emerges when rights are destroyed. ✖

Jo-Ann Mort is a US-based journalist and poet

 If it takes a village to raise a child, it takes a village, too, to keep a teenager safe

51(02):106/106|DOI:10.1177/03064220221110798